MW01200038

JANE DOE'S RETURN

JEN TALTY

JUPITER PRESS

PRAISE FOR JEN TALTY

Jane Doe's Return is a winner of The Beacon and The Molly writing contests.

"*Jane Doe's Return* is a gripping story full of suspense and mystery that will get your blood pumping and your mind churning." Long and Short Reviews

"*A blend of romance and suspense that kept me riveted!*" Christine Wenger, Bestselling Author

"*A charming setting and a steamy couple heat up the pages in an suspenseful story I couldn't put down!*" NY Times and USA today Bestselling Author Donna Grant.

Grab a glass of vino, kick back, relax, and let the romance roll in…

Sign up for my Newsletter (https://dl.bookfunnel.com/82gm8b9k4y) where I often give away free books before publication.

Join my private Facebook group (https://www.facebook.com/groups/191706547909047/) where I post exclusive excerpts and discuss all things murder and love!

BOOK DESCRIPTION

Imagine dedicating your entire career to finding the one person who can unlock the mystery behind your sister's murder—only to discover her in the last place you'd expect: as your new partner.

Special Agent Travis Brown has spent years building his career to gain access to the leads and information that might bring him closer to solving his sister's case. But nothing prepares him for Special Agent Shauna Morgan. With sharp instincts and undeniable beauty, Shauna quickly earns his respect—and sparks a powerful attraction that rivals his obsession with justice.

But Shauna has a secret, one that could shatter everything Travis thought he knew about his sister's death. As they navigate the gritty streets of Albany and the breathtaking landscapes of Lake George, they're drawn into a deadly game where every move puts Shauna's life—and Travis's heart—on the line.

Jane Doe's Return is a gripping contemporary romantic suspense that explores the courage to face the past and the risks of trusting someone who may hold the key to everything.

Special Agent Travis Brown entered the old hotel in downtown Albany, New York through the main doors, ignoring the putrid odor filling his nostrils. Rotted old hotels always smelled like urine-soaked clothing left in the sun for days. He took mental notes of anything, everything, as he scanned every inch of the lobby. Even a scrunched-up piece of paper, tossed carelessly in the corner, could be the clue that would lead them in the right direction. A cool sweat dampened his hairline. His hand trembled as he ran his fingers through his black hair. It was happening again.

The dull orange carpet felt like concrete as he made his way down the hall. He forced himself to focus as he nodded to the two uniformed city cops standing at attention outside the room where the body had been found.

Without saying a word, Travis flashed his badge.

"Who called in the FBI?" one of the officers questioned.

"Part of the Tri-City Task Force," Travis said.

"Great. Another bureaucrat decided to create more red tape just so they can make a name for themselves while we get blamed for killers running amok."

"Just doing my job, like you." If Travis didn't have ulterior motives, he would be able to understand the chest pounding. "What can you tell me?"

"The call came in around ten this evening," the officer said. "Detective Hutchensen is in charge. Why don't you talk to him?"

"I'll do that." Travis studied the crime scene, looking for anything that he might be able to connect to Marie's case. While this scene wasn't identical to his sister's, there were some similarities Travis couldn't dismiss. The gnawing voice in the back of his mind told him whoever killed this young girl had also killed Marie.

Travis snapped the latex gloves in place. The sudden impact of rubber against his skin shot the powdery lining into the air. He inhaled sharply, letting the powder linger in his nostrils, masking the scent of death. His stomach lurched in one violent motion to the back of his throat. He couldn't shake the feeling that the killer was somewhere watching him, mocking him.

The body lay face up on the bed. A pale-blue dress had been draped over the side, and a tiara rested above the victim's head. A bright light from a camera flashed across the room as the forensics team took pictures and moved about in an all too familiar pattern. "Detective Hutchensen, long time no see."

"Guess I shouldn't be surprised to see you here."

"My night to be out with the crazies."

"Can't say I'm all too happy about this task force thing. Just makes my job more difficult. This is why we have jurisdictions and all that," Hutchensen said.

"We've all got the same goal in mind. Besides, I was called in by your boss."

"Yeah, I know." Hutchensen could be a hard ass and liked doing things his way, but he was a damn good cop. Besides, Travis had to agree, sometimes joint forces only added confusion to a case. Too many cooks in the kitchen, so to speak.

"We're just looking for a profile on this one," Hutchensen said. "While it appears random, the scene looks ritualistic." He rose from his crouched position, standing about two inches taller than Travis's six-foot frame. "As you know, we've got a couple of open murder cases we're trying to connect. This one almost looks like a copycat of Matt Williams."

Travis cringed at the name. This was no copycat. This was the real deal. "I'll take a look around, run it through our national database." Travis was grateful for the chance to look at the crime scene firsthand.

Usually he viewed pictures and reports after the fact, trying to find a pattern to help form a profile of possible suspects, but this one fit a particular criminal, one that had been haunting Travis for years.

He made notes of similarities and differences between this crime scene, any unsolved case, and his sister's case. There had to be a clue. A hint. He couldn't afford to miss anything.

"Medical examiner is here," someone said from the hall.

"He can take the body," Hutchensen said. "Let's get all the evidence bagged and get out of here." He glanced over his shoulder at Travis. "Got anything off the cuff?"

Travis shook his head. "My instincts tell me there is more than meets the eye on this one." God, did he want first dibs on this case.

"I'll take what I can get."

Travis stepped from the hotel room, knowing his sister's killer had just struck again, but he couldn't prove it. His boss would blow a gasket if Travis tried to tie these scenes together without concrete evidence. With a heavy heart, Travis got in his truck and headed back to his apartment.

The empty back streets echoed the darkness in Travis's soul. He pulled into his driveway and then slammed the gearshift into park. He glanced at the small patch of grass with colorful bushes lining the side of the duplex. When would it all end? Recently, his mother had told him that his normally full-of-life blue eyes had turned dull and dead. He felt dead inside. The more years that passed, the more his heart yearned for closure. Real closure.

Once inside, he tossed his keys on the countertop in the kitchen and checked his voicemail. One message was from his mother and the other from Jake Hanson indicating he would be in town and would stop by soon. *Great.* Jake had probably already heard about the murder and wanted to check up on Travis.

He headed for his bedroom. He laid his coat on the neatly made bed, then went to his closet and shed his suit, making sure to hang up the pants. He tucked his shirt into his dry cleaning bag before pulling out his portable filing cabinet. Routine had been the only thing that kept him sane all these years.

He set all the unofficial files he had collected across his bed and took in a deep breath as he opened his laptop and connected to the FBI database. Somehow, he had to connect them. He had to prove that this particular killer was still walking the streets.

But try as he might, he couldn't make a concrete connection. Too many differences, not enough evidence. He searched for other possible connections with any active case in the hopes of pulling this murder into the FBI's jurisdiction, but got nothing even remotely close.

His report for the local cops would include a criminal profile, but he would recommend they start with family and any lovers and continue on that path until they found the girl's killer. It wasn't the FBI's case, so Travis would have to back off.

With the morning sun peeking through the shade, he sat on his bed and held the Polaroid of the young, dead girl. She had been only fourteen, the daughter of a prominent businessman, and only a year younger than his sister when she had been murdered.

Travis flipped open another file. The badly beaten and swollen face of a nameless girl called to him. He glided his fingers across the picture. Jane Doe had survived, but no one knew who she was or where she went. How did a fourteen-year-old disappear from a crime scene without a trace? The police hadn't gotten the chance to fingerprint her. They'd barely gotten the chance to talk to her before she slipped away into the night and hadn't been heard from since.

The police had never officially given up their search for Jane Doe, but after Matt Williams was charged with Marie's rape and death, they put the search on the back burner. They had enough evidence to convict Williams on multiple murders. Therefore, Jane Doe became immaterial. Williams would face life in prison. Yet the murders continued. Some fit the MO, others not so much, but Travis knew in his heart of hearts the killer was still out there searching for his next victim.

Regardless of what the rest of the world thought, Matt Williams didn't kill Travis's sister, and he didn't rape Jane Doe. These two things Travis would bet his life on. Finding Jane Doe had to be the answer. She was the one person who held the key to unlocking the mystery of a ruthless killer.

"Who are you? And where are you now?"

*T*ravis pulled into the parking garage of the Albany Federal Building after a sleepless night of staring at dead girls. He didn't think the week could get any worse. Until he got his mail with the letter denying his request.

He'd been banking on this promotion ever since his mentor and partner had moved up the ranks. They had to do something with him, so he figured he was a shoo-in. He grabbed a cup of coffee and headed down the hallway to his office.

He sat down behind his desk, squeezed the empty envelope tight, and then lifted it over his head. As if it were a basketball, he banked the crumpled piece of paper off the wall, but it missed the garbage can. "Damn."

He lifted his legs and plopped his feet on his desk. With his hands clasped behind his head, he leaned back in his chair and stared at the ceiling. Twelve pictures looked back at him.

"We need to talk," a voice from the hallway said. Scott Grimshaw, Special Agent in Charge and Travis's boss, leaned against the doorjamb.

Travis's feet hit the floor. "I'm listening."

"I read your report. Thanks for not putting a personal twist on things."

"The killer from last night wasn't some kind of copycat, nor was it a random act, but my gut doesn't constitute a lead in the direction I think we should take, even if I trust my gut."

"I, too, believe it wasn't a random act, but Marie's killer is behind bars," Scott said.

"Then why do we have all these open cases that are so damn similar with no real leads?"

"Because you read too much into things. Look, you're a good agent, let's focus on what we can do, not what haunts us."

"That is exactly what I'm doing," Travis said, averting his eyes to the piece of paper lying on his office floor. "Got my denial today."

"I know. I'm sorry."

"I shouldn't ask, but what did your letter say?"

"I gave you a glowing recommendation, but truthfully, I don't think you're ready yet."

"Thanks for the honesty." Truthfulness was the one thing Travis could always count on from his boss.

"You've only been with us for four years. It typically takes six or eight to get that position. Trust me. You'll get it eventually." Scott looked sympathetic; then again, he always appeared empathetic. Travis chalked it up to his silver-gray hair, which made him appear about ten years older than his actual age of about fifty. "You're a good agent, but we need you here," Scott said.

Travis said nothing. *Eventually* wasn't good enough. He stood and looked out over McCarty Avenue and watched the cars and people mindlessly move about their day.

"You've been assigned a first," Scott said, tossing a file on his desk.

"What?" Travis whipped his head around.

"She's got a—"

"A first *and* a skirt? You've got to be kidding me." He didn't mind the skirt part, but training a new agent could delay his promotion by two years, at least.

"Shauna Morgan. You know her?" Scott asked, still leaning against the wooden doorframe.

Travis wondered if he ever wore anything other than a dark-blue suit and a standard gray tie that damn near matched his eyes. "Can't say that I do." He rolled the name around in his brain, trying to place it but got nothing. "Why?"

"She's from the area, and a rape victim advocate, so I figured you might know her."

"Nope. Can't say I've ever heard of her." Travis scooped up the folder and thumbed through the papers until he came across his new partner's photo. For a brief moment, he held his breath. Standard FBI identification photographs were generally worse than mug shots, but his new partner, with her soft-looking brown hair and sparkling blue eyes was more than a looker.

"Doesn't matter. She's been assigned to this office because she fits the same profile as you."

"And what, pray tell, is that?" Travis asked.

"She's being tracked for the National Violent Crimes Unit."

"Oh, great. So she'll get the promotion before I do."

Scott let out a small chuckle. The man was too easily amused. "You are such a pessimist. If you two work together all nice, they'll transfer you as partners. It's preferred that way, you know."

"Yeah, yeah. Whatever you say." Travis was having a hard time buying the line of bullshit his boss was dishing out. Besides, he wasn't a pessimist. If that were the case, he would have given up on finding his sister's killer years ago. Cynical maybe. Pessimist, certainly not.

"You need to pick up your new partner at the airport this afternoon at five. Officially, she's on the job the moment you lay eyes on her. I expect you to train her better than your mentor trained you." Scott pointed to the ceiling with a disapproving look. "Which means those have to go."

Travis glanced up at the constant reminders of his biggest failure. He'd been told before to toss the pictures, but he never listened.

"Now. I can't have you training a new agent with closed cases, and cases the FBI isn't even involved in, on your ceiling. If you don't take them down, I will do it for you."

"Fine." Travis shrugged. One of these days, someone would have to listen to him.

"And keep Agent Morgan out of your own little investigation. You'll never get that promotion if I have to write you up."

Travis nodded. Scott had been somewhat understanding over the years, but Travis knew he'd been skating on thin ice when it came to how much he used his job to get information for himself.

"Agent Morgan's your shadow. You don't go to the bathroom without her."

Travis gave a grunt of acceptance, climbing on top of his desk. He figured Scott would stick around until he pulled the pictures down.

Travis jumped down, and Scott strode out of the office. Travis put the pictures of twelve teenage victims, all raped and murdered but one, into a folder. Holding Jane Doe's picture in his hand, he stared at her bruised face. He stroked the picture and put it into a file, then shoved it in his top drawer. Time to meet his new partner.

*S*hauna Morgan gasped, then gripped the armrests, grateful no one was sitting in the seat next to her. The plane shook as the ground appeared to rise up from nowhere and greet the spinning wheels. The ones she prayed had been deployed, released, or whatever.

She hated flying but had to look out the window. It seemed everyone who feared flying had to fixate their stare on the approaching ground. Like watching yourself plummet to your death would somehow make your trip better.

The plane bounced on the pavement, came to a roaring halt, and jerked forward toward the gate. She tried to swallow, but the lump in her throat wouldn't allow her muscles to work properly. Her heart beat so fast she could no longer feel one pulse after the other. It had been years since she had been anywhere near her hometown. Although Saratoga Springs was about forty minutes north, Albany was close enough.

And Albany was where it all began.

She shook her hands, trying to get rid of her nerves before adjusting her brown hair. She wondered if she should have pulled it into a ponytail. Making a good first impression was more than important. Working at the Albany Field Office had been a dream come true, but to be working with Travis had been almost too much to handle all at once. She'd spent the majority of her adult life making sure she dealt with her past so she could use it to make sure the man who changed her life forever would pay. And pay big.

Travis would know some of what Shauna had suffered since the same man who had raped Shauna and almost stole her very essence had murdered his sister. Lucky for her, she'd been born a fighter and took advantage of every free and confidential counseling session she could find within the system of public and private education. It had taken every ounce of courage she could muster to push past all the pain and despair, but somehow she managed to come out on top. She planned on staying there.

She squeezed her blue eyes shut tight. Her therapist once told her that her eyes gave away every thought. It was game on now, and she had to make sure her past didn't bite her in the ass. There was always the chance Travis believed the police had captured, and the law had convicted, the right man, but Shauna didn't believe Matt Williams had killed Marie Brown. Shauna may not have been able to identify her attacker's face, but she did remember his voice. She'd never forget that voice. It still echoed in her ears.

The plane bucked to a stop, and Shauna opened her eyes. She pushed her hair back in hopes it would fall over the front of her shoulders again. She didn't wear much makeup, so she didn't bother checking it. She knew she looked put together, but wouldn't stand out, which was exactly what she wanted. No attention.

Just another woman in a sea of people moving from one place to the next.

Lights flickered, and the other passengers scurried to their feet. She stood, grabbed her purse and overnight bag, and headed down the tight path toward the door. The flight attendant smiled politely, and Shauna couldn't help but wonder why anyone in their right mind would fly for the fun of it.

She squared her shoulders and took in a deep breath. Her new boss had called stating Agent Brown would pick her up, but she wasn't ready to face him. She needed to figure out a way to get Travis to talk about his sister without giving away her own secret. If anyone knew who she was, she'd be transferred quicker than a bullet ripping through a bull's-eye hole at the range.

Or worse. She'd be thrown out of the FBI before she had a chance to catch the man who put her in this line of work to begin with. She'd been thrilled the day she heard about the impending trial of Matt Williams, suspected of killing at least five girls, but when she heard his voice on the news, she knew her nightmare hadn't ended. Worse, future victims were out there, unaware of their fate. From that moment, she'd made the decision to do whatever was necessary to stop living in fear and use what happened to her, and the energy it created, for a greater purpose. She had set out to help others, but soon realized it would be her calling to find Travis, and then find her attacker.

During her education and training in the FBI, she focused on victims of violent crimes and their attackers. She knew all too well what these victims had suffered, but she also knew with a little help, they could move past it and have a fulfilling life, if they chose to. Her goal was to work at the national level dealing with tracking down violent offenders and helping their victims. The Albany office was a stepping-stone to her ultimate goal, so she was truly grateful for the assignment. It meant her superiors trusted her abilities since Travis was on the same track.

She glanced one last time at his picture. He wore his jet-black hair a little longer than most of the FBI agents she knew. And the way he styled it...well, he overdid it a bit. Kind of like all those pretty boy pop singers that graced the pages of magazines. His deep-blue eyes, even in a picture, touched her soul, but she could still see the pain looming behind the brilliant blue pools.

She scanned the airport terminal, trying to ignore the smell of bad feet. Why did all airports smell like the world walked around without socks on? At first glance, she didn't see Agent Brown, but a second look around and...there he was.

He leaned against the wall with a newspaper in his hands. His legs were crossed at the ankles, and his eyes appeared to shift as if he were reading the paper. It seemed Special Agent Brown was trying to blend in, almost hiding from her. Had she not seen his picture, she would have walked right by him.

"Agent Brown?" she asked, lifting her chin. By no means was she short, but she had to tilt her head to look him in the eye.

"You must be Agent Morgan." He folded the paper and then placed it on top of the trash receptacle next to him.

"Please, call me Shauna." She held out her hand and fought the urge to look him over. Attractive men were a dime a dozen, besides, she had a job to do.

"The name's Travis." He took her hand in a firm grip. She liked that, but she was unnerved by the way her hand felt in his. She looked down just as he yanked his hand away. "It's a pleasure. Luggage?" He pointed toward the sign that read 'Baggage Claim.'

She fell in line with his long stride. Damn, his legs were longer than hers, and she had an inseam that most fancy designers didn't know existed.

"Where'd we put you up?"

"I've got it here somewhere." She dug into her purse. "It's on Wolfe Road, I think," she said, trying to keep up. "Some kind of residence inn or something."

He chuckled. "They put me there, too, but it only lasted a few nights. Not the best place. Basically, it's a glorified hotel. Have you started to look for a more permanent place to live?" He leaned against a pole in the middle of the baggage claim area and made eye contact.

She wondered if she hadn't known about his sister if she would be able to read the sorrow seeping from his intense stare. "I grew up in Saratoga, so I know Albany pretty well."

He lifted a brow, and the right corner of his mouth tipped in a half-smile.

She tried not to smile back, but she liked his personality: the strong quiet type. Not overly confident, but charismatic, and somewhat sensitive. Or at least that was what she sensed. "I don't like complex living, so I'm looking for a duplex or something," she added for lack of anything better. She eyed her suitcases coming down the conveyer belt and reached for them.

He snatched the first one from her, and subsequently, the other two.

"Thanks," she said, hoping she hadn't pegged him wrong. He didn't seem like the typical arrogant type, but then again, most agents were a little bit on the self-centered side.

"Not a problem." He smiled over his shoulder and continued out the doors toward what appeared to be his illegally parked truck. With ease, he raised her suitcases and slid them across the tailgate, then opened the door for her. After tucking her into the passenger seat, he leapt around the front and slipped into the driver's side, then handed her a file.

"What's this?"

"A rape case I need another set of eyes on. Hungry?"

"Not if we're going to be discussing rape while we're eating." She placed the file in her lap, resisting the urge to dive right into whatever case the man was working on. She took a deep breath and reminded herself of how her professors would constantly harp on her to slow down and stop trying to figure everything out in the first pass. That patience and attention to detail were the key to knowledge.

Even her therapists had cautioned her to stop trying to fix or do everything in one day or in one pass. Healing would take time, and even those who were committed to recovery and living with whatever it was that hurt them needed to take their time in coping with the past, present, and even the future.

"Well, we might be discussing a lot of ugly stuff while we're eating. Does that bother you?"

"No. I've been told I'm too focused. Too much on the job. I need to learn how to separate my career from my life."

He laughed. "Me, too. Do you like pizza?" He glanced at her and then pulled off the road. "Capri's has the best pizza in town."

"Pizza sounds good to me." She went to open the door, but he jumped out, and in two strides beat her to it. "Thank you, but I'm completely capable of opening my own door." She was going to have to do something about his apparent need to take care of her as if she were incapable.

"I'm sure you are." He opened the door into the restaurant for her, too.

She smiled politely, but she wanted him to treat her like an equal. Seen for her mind, not her looks.

He smiled and waved to at least a half-dozen people. It seemed he knew just about everyone in the restaurant. That made her uneasy. For years, she had avoided this area, and with good reason. Now she simply wanted to blend in. She didn't think coming back would be so hard. However, knowing her attacker could be out there, waiting for her return, sent a shiver up her spine.

She glanced around the small but quaint bar and grill. Booths lined the right side and tables were set down the middle. The left side housed the bar. She noted everyone in the place, who they were with, and what they were wearing. Even if her attacker were here, she wouldn't recognize him. He had drugged her, and she never got a good look at his face.

Part of her wanted to tell Travis who she was, but not until she was sure he believed that Marie's killer was still walking the streets. Patience, she reminded herself. She also had to make sure he'd continue to keep her identity from their superiors. She had come too far, endured too much. It wasn't so much about catching this bastard herself anymore, but she truly believed she had something to offer the violent crimes unit, specifically when it came to rape. "I appreciate the kindness, but I'm your partner. You don't have to open doors and carry my things."

The corner of his mouth tilted. "Shauna, I understand. Really I do, but I can't help it." He waved the waitress over.

"Hey, Trav. What's up?" A cute, young blonde bounced over with two glasses of water in her hands. She smiled, making Shauna feel even more out of place. She adjusted her shirt collar, brushing her hair behind her shoulders.

"Hi, Bonnie. The usual for me. Shauna?" Travis shifted his eyes from Bonnie to her.

"What's the usual?"

"Diet Coke with a lemon." He flashed a grin.

"Same for me," Shauna said.

"If it were after eight, he'd order a beer. Only one." Bonnie patted his head. "But he's a good tipper."

"Hey! Watch the hair." He swatted her hand away.

"I'll bring the Cokes over and put an order in for pizza. You like sausage?" Bonnie looked at Shauna.

"Sausage and pepperoni." Shauna glanced at Travis, who nodded. Damn, the man was way too agreeable. She wondered what he would have done if she had ordered anchovies or maybe some vegetarian pizza.

"Keep an eye on this one and make sure he's being a gentleman," Bonnie added playfully.

As if he'd be anything else.

"This is my new partner," he clarified.

Well, at least he used the word partner. Score one for Travis.

"Wow. Female agent. Very cool. Glad it's not a date. You're definitely way too classy." Bonnie grinned over her shoulder as she swayed away.

"Since we are on the subject of being partners, I'd like to discuss something with you." Shauna took a sip of water, thinking about how to set the ground rules. She needed to gain his trust and learn from him. Not just about her job, but about what he knew and how he could help her. "Specifically, being treated as an equal."

"For the record, I had a woman partner when I was with the New York City Police Department. She hated it when anyone treated her differently, but she never minded me being a gentleman," he said, seemingly amused.

Fool was too cute for his own good. Or maybe hers.

"What does that mean?" She wiped the dew from her water glass.

"It means you being a woman has nothing to do with your ability as an agent, but everything to do with the fact that I'm a gentleman." He tipped his glass to her and then smiled, showing off his straight, white teeth before lifting the drink to his lips.

The pizza arrived with perfect timing. She needed to digest his words, but until she got to know him on a more professional level, she would reserve her opinion and choose her words more carefully.

Her identity would stay a secret until he showed her he believed the real killer still lurked behind a shadow. Waiting for her.

2

After dinner, Shauna followed Travis back to his pickup. The crisp air did nothing to settle her nerves. She scanned the city streets, hoping Travis didn't notice her trembling hands.

"I can't change this habit, but trust me, I know who you are," he said as he opened the door.

Her muscles tensed, and she paused. He knew nothing; and yet, he probably knew everything. An uneasy feeling washed over her as she settled into the passenger seat and he in the driver's seat.

"How about you take a look at that file?" He pulled out into traffic and headed toward Wolfe Road, where the temporary housing was located.

"I'd almost forgotten." She reached for the file, brushing his hand as he went for it at the same time. She looked over at him. "Umm, let me see." She fumbled with the papers, not liking the effect he seemed to have on her as a woman.

"Why don't we sit down and look at it together?" His voice calmed her, which made her more uncomfortable.

He pulled into a parking lot.

"Thought this was a temporary housing unit or something?"

"The units are all basically mini-apartments used by our department and some major corporations. It's not that bad," he said with a slight smile.

She checked herself in, and they made their way down the dimly lit hallway toward her room.

"Okay. What's the problem with this case?" she asked, after he pushed back the door. Her new surroundings didn't do much for her, so working seemed like a much better plan.

"Not sure," Travis said, then stopped and glanced over his shoulder, shrugging. "Really, I've seen worse."

Looking around her new living space, she tried to tell herself Travis had a point. The hideous, sagging brown couch that was pushed back against the not-so-white wall could be spruced up with a brightly colored cover. She remembered a flower shop they'd passed and figured the ugly Sixties' throwback table might look quite homey with some fresh mixed flowers, really scented ones, because the musty aroma in the room choked her.

"They're going to do renovations soon." Travis

tossed her key on the table and took her suitcases to an open door. "The bedroom doesn't get any better." He left her suitcases by the door, then turned. "You got the file?"

"Oh, yeah." She spread the file on the kitchen table before sitting down across from him. She shuffled the papers over the flat surface, then blew out a puff of air and tried to concentrate. As she scanned the initial police report, her heart hammered behind her rib cage. She knew this case. Well, not exactly, but based on what she could gather, she knew whoever killed this young girl had tried to kill her, too.

She did her best to keep her heart rate as flat as possible as excitement pulsed through her veins. It wasn't the kind of excitement that made her feel good, but in some ways, it gave her strength. Not only had she been given her dream job, but now her rapist had been handed to her on a silver platter. She would study this man. This rapist. Murderer. Find his weak spot and put an end to his terror. It wouldn't end there. So many other victims cried for justice, and she'd do her best to give it to them—all of them.

Twenty minutes ticked by as she did her best to concentrate on the file, and not her own emotional roller-coaster ride. She was a full-fledged agent now, and she needed to behave like one on all levels. She reminded herself that this was no longer about what happened to her, but catching a killer, plain and simple.

Travis didn't really say anything to her, just pretended not to watch her. The hair on the back of her neck prickled. She asked a few questions and studied the case, keeping herself as detached as possible.

Lifting two pictures in the air, she compared them. In one picture, the victim's head was tilted just to the left. The same angle had been used for the second picture, but the head appeared to be straight. Then she noticed a safety pin pressed deep in the green shag carpet in the first picture, but the pin wasn't in the second one.

Taking a deep breath, she brought her focus back to the pictures. Not only had the crime scene been tampered with, but this case was older than she thought. She swallowed, knowing others had died.

"That's it." She nudged his arm.

"Huh?" He took the pictures and looked at them.

She rubbed her hands on her slacks and pointed to the safety pin.

"I can't believe I didn't see that before."

She sat back in her chair and folded her arms across her chest. "Yeah, right."

"What do you see?" he questioned with a straight face.

"I think you know what I see," she said, frustrated.

"Tell me." He pushed the pictures in front of her.

"The crime scene was tampered with after the initial photographs were taken." She flipped over the pictures and pointed to the times written on the back. "And this case is about eight years old." She tried to swallow, unsure of what her next move should be. Clearly her skills were being put to the test, but why this case?

"The guy charged with the case was put away, but not for this murder. Too many things were disturbed at the scene to pin it on him, not to mention the unprofessional way the evidence was treated. To make matters worse, there were no other suspects. Case closed on a technicality." He turned his chair and leaned back, clasping his hands behind his head.

She knew Travis had to have personal feelings attached to this particular case. She shoved the pictures aside, desperately trying to keep the flashes of the past from interfering with the present. "So, did I pass?"

He gave a slight smile.

"That was a little underhanded."

"My job is to train you. If I presented this as a test, you would have approached it differently, instead of using your instincts. Which, by the way, are damn good." He stood and stretched.

When he twisted his back to the side, she let her eyes drop, then blushed.

"I'd better get going. We have a court date at nine."

She led the way to the door, thinking about her partner in ways that would most likely be considered unprofessional. Compartmentalize, she reminded herself. Keep each detail of her life in its appropriate box and all would be good. "We do?"

His long fingers squeezed her upper arm, sending a pulse down her body. Stiffening her spine, she forced the physical sensations to the side and concentrated on her mission. The only way Travis fit in the picture was through the information he could provide. Her attraction to the man would just interfere with not only her career goals, but her personal goals as well.

Abruptly, he pulled his hand away. "Never a dull moment. I'll pick you up at seven forty-five. Goodnight."

"Thanks." She closed the door and took in a deep breath, looking around at an apartment that had little to offer. "I can do this." She blinked a few times. The same faceless man who had been haunting her mind for years laughed at her. "I'm coming for you," she whispered. The only way she knew how to close the door on her past was to find the guy who had nearly destroyed her.

---

*T*ravis pulled down his street, noticing an extended cab pickup sitting in his driveway. "Great." He parked next to Jake Hanson's truck. "What brings you by?"

"Working a dumbass case for some rich chick."

Jake stepped from his vehicle and stretched out his tattoo-covered arm. "Heard about the latest murder."

"I bet you did," Travis said. "It's late. I've got court in the morning."

"Won't stay long. One beer and enough time to make myself presentable before I head home." Jake threw his hands wide and grinned.

"Fine." Travis headed for his apartment. "You really need a shave."

"Yeah. The wife will have a cow if I go home like this. Not to mention the little princess of the house won't greet her daddy with all this stubble. She says it's not good for her complexion or some such nonsense."

"How old is Katie?"

"Five, but she's very high maintenance." Jake laughed.

"Because you spoil the hell out of her." Travis pushed back his door and let Jake pass. The man was built like a tank but not very tall. Most people were afraid of him because of his gruff exterior, but he was a big softy. And a sap to boot. "I've got an extra razor. You can shower here if you want."

"Thanks." Jake made himself at home by snagging a couple of beers from the refrigerator and sitting down in Travis's favorite chair. Then Jake kicked off his shoes and put his dirty, smelly feet on the coffee table.

"Why don't you shower first?"

"Okay." Jake guzzled his beer before thankfully heading to the bathroom. "I've been doing surveillance for about three days now."

"Yeah. I can smell it."

Travis tossed Jake a few towels and then headed to his room. He stood on his bed and taped the pictures of the girls from his office to his bedroom ceiling. Never again would he allow himself to lose focus.

After all the pictures were in place, he laid down, resting his head on his pillows and stared at the constant reminders. He hadn't learned anything new by showing an old case to his new partner, except that his partner was probably smarter than him. It certainly hadn't constituted a test, not in the eyes of his employer, but having a different set of eyes always helped add perspective, especially when there was no bias attached to her viewpoint. However, it still proved to be a futile attempt at trying to find the missing piece.

"What the fuck are you doing?" Jake's voice boomed across the room. "Anyone ever tell you that you're weird?" Jake glanced at the ceiling.

"All the damn time."

"Does the murder from the other night fit into your theory?" Jake stood at the foot of the bed.

"You almost look like a normal, upstanding guy," Travis said.

"Don't change the subject. I know you."

Travis understood Jake's concern. He'd seen Travis in some of his darkest hours. "Some of the case fits. There are so many inconsistencies, but that's the least of my problems right now."

"Yeah, I heard about the no-go on the promotion."

"You talk to my family way too much."

Jake laughed. "What's bugging you, besides the same old shit?"

"Got a new partner."

"And?"

"A first and a skirt."

"Nice," Jake said.

Agent Morgan had been a little more than Travis had bargained for. The moment he spied her at the airport, she'd had an effect on him. And not just his brain. Not a great way to start a partnership.

She'd impressed him by knowing exactly who he was, without him having to approach her. She hadn't been timid in her approach or in her demeanor. Shauna Morgan had proven herself to be one smart lady. She knew within five minutes that something wasn't right with the case he'd presented. He hadn't planned on giving her that test until they were in the office. And certainly not with that case. He told himself it had all been about trust—the key element in being good partners—and it had to come quickly.

"What? No comeback?"

"Thinking, that's all."

"Either you're letting your obsession rule your overactive mind, or this skirt has you thinking with the other brain."

"Neither. Just a long day."

"Bullshit," Jake said, leaning against the wall. "Is there something wrong with your new partner?"

Travis did his best not to smile. Shauna had accused him of being underhanded. If she only knew. He'd been tested with a textbook case, not a case his superior had been secretly working on. Was he so desperate to find his sister's killer that he'd bring in his new partner without letting her know what he was doing?

"Not a damn thing wrong with her." He frowned. "She's smart and sexy as hell."

Now, that could be a problem. Agent Morgan had...well, she had caught his attention.

He conjured up a picture of Shauna. She carried herself with poise and confidence. She dressed professionally, pulling her light-brown hair away from her face and wearing just enough makeup that she didn't look like she had to try too hard to be pretty. Probably not at all.

"So, you've got the hots for your new partner," Jake said. "Better than thinking she's a dumbass."

"There is something different about her."

"Uh-huh."

"What's that supposed to mean?"

"I haven't seen you get bent out of shape over a woman, ever. Your family worries that you'll never open your heart. I worry that when you do, it will get ripped to shreds."

"You're an ass, you know that?"

"Just a friend who's got your back." Jake sipped his beer, looking at the girls on the ceiling. "Don't bring your new partner into all this."

"What makes you think I'd do that?"

"Because you think she's smarter than you, which means you'll do anything to get her opinion."

Travis pictured Shauna's light-blue eyes. They looked like she carried some kind of burden behind them. His instincts told him she had a secret; other than that, he couldn't find one thing he didn't like about her.

"You're about as smart as they come, and I wouldn't do anything to get your opinion."

"That's because I'm easy."

"Yeah, you are." Travis laughed.

"Want me to do some digging around this last case?"

"What have you found out already?" Travis knew Jake wouldn't wait to be asked, he'd just do it the way he did everything. A trait he admired and resented at the same time.

"Not much. Cops are looking at the boyfriend,

who is as clean as a whistle according to their records. I watched his patterns, and he's definitely hiding something, but I don't think he killed the girl."

"I know he didn't." Travis rose, stood on the bed, and pointed to the latest victim. "That's her." Travis moved his finger to his sister's picture. "Marie was killed in the same manner. If they make any connection, it will be some copycat thing."

"It happens all the time."

Travis tapped his finger on Jane Doe. "She knows the answers. I have to find her."

Jake let out a long breath. "That path is so cold even I can't pick it up anymore."

"Maybe my new partner can."

"Keep your ass out of trouble, would you? Let me do your dirty work. At least I have an excuse," Jake said. "If she's new, you're supposed to train her, not teach her how to become obsessed with closed cold cases."

"It's going to be a long two years."

---

*T*he second knock on Shauna's door came a few minutes after the first. "I'm coming!" she yelled from the bathroom. "Punctual, too," she muttered to herself, taking one last glance in the mirror. "Not bad." She squared her shoulders and headed for the living area.

She pulled open the door and found herself checking Travis out. Not a single hair on his head was out of place. He looked damn spiffy in a suit and tie, too. Another time. Or place. Different circumstances. Well, she'd be all over Travis Brown. His good looks matched his intelligence, and then some.

He glanced at his watch when he opened the door of his pickup.

"I'm not late...you're early." He might be good-looking, but he would drive her nuts with this *early* thing.

"Yeah, well, my mother taught me fifteen minutes early is on time, five minutes early is late." He flashed a grin and strolled to the other side of the truck.

"I'm not your mother; I'm your partner." She made eye contact, hoping to make her point very clear.

"I've noticed."

"Good. Next time be late."

"I'll work on it."

Moments later, they settled themselves in the back row of the city courtroom. The defendant was a thirty-year-old white male accused of raping an elderly woman. The prosecuting attorney spent an enormous amount of time going over the gruesome details of the case. He even showed pictures. Shauna's stomach began to flip as if she were on an amusement ride.

She didn't know what was worse—raping young

girls or old women. Her uncanny ability to compartmentalize everything in her life was being threatened. She had to find a way to keep her fears from interfering with her job. Her stomach gurgled like a volcano about to erupt. In order to keep her thoughts from the acid hitting her throat, she glanced around the courtroom to find something to fix her stare on. She landed her attention on how nicely Travis filled out a suit. It seemed to calm her stomach.

The Assistant D.A. called Travis to the stand, and Shauna's pulse quickened. He rose and took long, confident strides to the witness stand. Looking at him with one hand on the Bible and the other in the air, swearing to tell the whole truth and nothing but the truth, the butterflies in her stomach fluttered about like she was some pathetic teenager with a silly crush. She blinked, forcing herself to remember why she was sitting in the courtroom.

His smooth smoky voice sent a tingle down her spine and commanded her to hang on his every word. He answered every question with an air of assurance that even if he was lying, she suspected everyone would believe him.

Travis glided down the aisle, taking her by the elbow and pulling her along with him.

"Why are we leaving?" she whispered.

"Because we're done."

"But the case? It's not over." She pointed back at the courthouse. "I want to know—"

"Our job is done. I gave my expert testimony, the facts as I knew them. The rest is out of my hands."

"But don't you want to know what the jury comes back with?"

Travis paused near the main door of the courthouse. "Of course I do. However, the verdict could be hours, or days, away."

"I understand that, but based on your testimony, you've already put a good chunk of your own time on this case. There is other testimony to be heard and closing arguments. I figured it would be not only important to you, but our department, for you to see it all the way through."

"If they need me back, they'll call. Until then, we have other work to do." Travis glanced at his cell phone. "Besides, something is up." Travis held her elbow and guided her through the sea of cars in the parking lot. "We need to check in with the boss."

"Kind of strange. I haven't met him yet, only talked to him on the phone a few times. What's he like?" His hand felt warm through her blazer, and his gentle touch gave her comfort. She took a step back as his hand fell to his side.

"Scott? He's a stickler for the rulebook. More importantly, he likes things done his way and on his timeline, which brings me to the fact he's called three times." Travis smiled. "He's also very impatient so I'd best call him back, pronto." Travis flipped his cell open and opened the truck door, motioning for her to get in. "What's up..." He paused. "We're on our way." He snapped the phone shut, jumped in the pickup, and started driving. He didn't say another word.

"Are you going to tell me where we're going and why?" She looked at him.

"Oh, sorry. We've been called to a crime scene as part of the Tri-City Joint Task Force."

"What kind of crime scene?"

"Murder."

She held her stomach and wondered if Marie's killer had struck again. The same man who had killed countless others. Who had almost killed her. But no one had a name for him, because he didn't really exist.

"You okay?" He squeezed her shoulder and then released her. His eyes stayed on the road.

"Just tired." She swallowed her emotions. This was it. Every moment she'd spent working on getting through the pain. Becoming a stronger, better person. Finding herself again. All of it led her to this moment in time.

"Sure that's it?"

"I'm fine," she said a little too tersely. She was anything but fine. Fear ripped through her bloodstream like a raging inferno.

"I was freaked out when I got called to my first murder scene. It's normal."

"Just a lot to take on the first day."

"You don't have to get too involved. Sit back, watch, and learn. This task force thing is new, so we're really only here to support the cops."

"So, this isn't our case?" Any case that would bring her closer to her rapist was one she wanted.

"Not sure yet. Right now, it falls under the jurisdiction of the locals, but depending on what we find, it could be, so we have to make sure we get a good look at the scene."

"I'm good with details."

The way he tilted his head as he glanced at her gave her the impression he wasn't sold on her abilities. Well, she'd have to simply prove him wrong.

***

*T*ravis rubbed his jaw and then stole a glance at Shauna. She sat stiff-backed in her seat, with her gaze focused out the windshield. She seemed to be lost in her own thoughts. Normally he could read most people with ease. He couldn't tell if she was merely organizing and preparing, as any good agent would, or mentally trying to block out any negative thoughts and images. As a cop, he'd been told to prepare and then mentally block. However, he had been unable to prepare until he went on his first call. No point in trying to tell her, she'd have to learn on her own.

He pulled up next to a sheriff's car. The tension in his body escalated, constricting his muscles to the point of pain. Okay, so they were both human, and he still had a hard time in the preparation department. "Just stick close to me." He nodded to her.

Travis circled the crime scene, doing his best to avoid contact with everyone until he got a good feel for what he was dealing with.

"Agent Brown," Detective Hutchensen said. "You seem to be following me around these days."

"So I do. Tell me what we've got."

"This one's a runaway. Parents admitted she had a long history with drug use. Probably a case of the wrong place at the wrong time. We're still trying to gather information on her from other sources, but it looks like she hung with a tough crowd. Probably find our perp there."

"You don't know that."

"Taking an educated guess."

"I don't like guessing," Travis said. Even though he would do his best to try to find a connection, any connection, to his sister's case, he'd learned long ago to keep an open mind during the information gathering process. In his early days, he'd been wrong before, spending too much time looking at cases from only one angle and he'd missed some important clues. A mistake he'd never make again.

Hutchensen chuckled. "Your job is about guessing."

"True, but I don't have enough valuable information to form a decent guess."

"You're always looking in one direction," Hutchensen said. Ignoring the comment, Travis snapped a glove in place and knelt in front of a lifeless form covered with a standard issue blanket. Over the years, he'd learned how to keep himself from trembling and his face from turning white every time he looked at a dead body. It didn't make it any easier. He swallowed. This crime scene didn't fit his sister's, but he knew deep in his gut this was the killer he'd been searching for his entire career. The only problem, why would his guy kill twice in the same year? He'd never done that before.

One kill on the same date. It never changed.

Until today.

Taking a deep breath, he drew back the blanket, and then heard a sharp intake of breath behind him.

The young victim had been bludgeoned beyond recognition. Travis closed his eyes briefly and then replaced the blanket. Shauna had already turned away.

"You okay?" he whispered in her ear. He remembered his first violent case. Didn't matter how well his training had prepared him, he could never shake any of the victim's images from his mind.

"Yeah. Just trying to organize everything I've seen so far." She pulled out a small note pad and scribbled in it. "Who was that guy you were talking to?"

"Detective Rosco Hutchensen. Good cop. Real good, but a pain in the ass."

"Did he have any details about the girl?"

"Nothing concrete, except the girl was into drugs and a possible runaway. He'll file a report by the end of the day and send it to us. We'll compare it to our findings, send over our thoughts, and it will probably stay with local." Before the joint task force, he'd done everything in his power to make up a reason why each murder should be the FBI's case. Now, with the shared information policy, he had greater access, although he had to be careful. Cops like Hutchensen didn't like all Travis's poking around.

"How long has she been missing?"

He noticed she wiped her face before she turned. When her eyes caught his, he sensed how she struggled to keep her own personal feelings at bay and deal with the situation at hand. Sometimes the job hardened people to the point they couldn't feel anything real anymore. He prayed that never happened to him. Or her. "About eight days. She'd gone missing before, so the exact day is off."

"The killer preys on young runaways. He finds their weakness and gains their trust. He promises them fame or freedom, whatever it is they're running from. He promises to protect them. Only to rape and murder them in the end."

"You want to tell me what you see here to make you draw that conclusion?" She had quoted him a textbook answer, and even if her conclusions were right on, there wasn't an ounce of evidence to back up her findings. Either she wasn't as smart as he thought, or she knew something he didn't.

He was banking on the latter.

She blinked and then looked around. "It's not so much what I see here, but all the facts put together."

"There are no facts. You're going by emotion, not fact." He touched the small of her back, edging her toward the truck.

"You heard the medical examiner, she was most likely beaten, raped, then bludgeoned to death. It's a well-known fact that rapists are generally repeat offenders."

"But we don't have enough evidence to go on any theory yet. It's important to close your mind off to what you think you know, or what makes sense. Bring things down to the simplest level. Do a full victimology report. Interview friends and family. Look over all the evidence at the crime scene and then start matching it up with what we know about rapists and murderers."

"I've done extensive research on just this type of victim and murderer. Some of my findings have been published."

"Impressive, but you can't let what you think you know interfere with what the crime scene tells you." He turned the key. "All I see is a girl who was beaten, raped, murdered, and left out here." He waved his hand toward the sky. "For all we know it was a relative, boyfriend, or—"

"Is that what you believe?" she asked, but it wasn't a question. She didn't believe it any more than he did.

"Those kinds of theories are best kept to yourself until you have concrete facts to back them up. There isn't a single law enforcement officer who'd base a case on what *you* think. As the old saying goes, 'just the facts, ma'am.' Collect the evidence and then prove your theory to yourself first." He paused and made eye contact. She wasn't a run-of-the-mill rookie, so her thoughts threw him. He'd expected more from her, but something told him she wasn't being forthright with all her thoughts, and he couldn't figure out why. "We don't know anything until we analyze the data and the victimology."

She cleared her throat. "How many girls?"

"'How many girls what?"

"This is a serial killer."

"We don't know that."

"But you think that is exactly what we're dealing with."

He would be hard-pressed to link this case to any that were still open. Maybe one, if he was lucky. "What I think is that we need to dig deeper before we go off half-cocked."

"You gave me a really old case file last night for a reason. Why? And don't tell me it was to test my ability to go over evidence secondhand."

Smart girl. How much could he trust her, and did he want to? He navigated the city streets while he collected his thoughts, thankful she was waiting patiently.

"This will make five cases the FBI is aiding the police in. Personally, I can't find a connection strong enough to link the victims to one killer. Victim patterns don't match up with the criminal patterns. So I guess the official answer would be this appears to be an isolated incident." Travis pulled into the parking garage.

She stared out the window. She looked as if the weight of the world sat on her shoulders, which he thought was an odd reaction to the conversation, even though she'd been thrown into the pits of hell on her first day.

"Nothing is ever as it appears to be. I don't think we can rule anything out."

"We're not. However, we can't jump to conclusions either."

"I understand."

"You okay?" he asked, just before he got out of the truck.

"Yeah." She pushed back the door. "I didn't expect to jump into the mind of a psychopath so quickly."

"The only time I like dealing with rapists is when I get to help put them away. Worst kind in my book." He didn't try to hide the edge in his voice. "Long day." He tried to smile but couldn't.

*T*he office welcome overwhelmed Shauna. Everyone she met had been more than gracious. Well, almost everyone. It seemed Special Agent Jeff Wilcox thought of women as objects, and nothing more. He'd been nice enough, but made it perfectly clear he had something else on his mind when he offered to show her the town.

Sitting in Special Agent Scott Grimshaw's office with Travis, she tried to focus on the conversation, but her mind kept drifting back to the recent murder and all the cases Travis had been trying to link together. How much did he know? More importantly, how could she get him to open up without making him suspicious of her motives?

"Shauna?" A hand squeezed her shoulder.

"Sorry." She coughed. "My mind is on the murder from this morning."

"I understand it's been a hectic day." Scott smiled. He reminded her of her college roommate's great uncle. A sweet, generous man who always seemed to understand, even if he didn't.

"If there is anything I can do, just let me know." Scott rose and shook her hand.

She liked Scott, not bad-looking for an older man, but even if he appeared to be the understanding boss, something in his detached demeanor toward Travis made her nervous. Maybe it was just being back in this city.

"Am I interrupting?" a voice from the hallway echoed.

"Not at all. Shauna, this is Steve Ramsey. I think he's about the only agent you haven't met yet."

Shauna shook Steve's hand. Something about him made the hair on her neck stand up. When she looked him in his gray eyes, it was like looking into a churning sea of anger. She jerked her hand back when he smiled. It was happening too fast. Her counselor was right, sometimes slow was better. She needed some time to adjust to her new surroundings and the idea that the rapist, *her rapist,* was so close he could reach out and touch her sent her pulse raging.

"Nice to meet you, Shauna. You look familiar. Have we met?"

She swallowed, reminding herself that lots of men had blond hair, and this man was an agent, not a raving lunatic. "I don't think so." She tried to put her best smile on as she allowed his voice to echo in her ears. She would've recognized the voice.

"Come on, Shauna. We still have a few things to cover today." Travis motioned to the door.

"Steve, you need to stay and go over this court decision with me," Scott said.

"No problem," Steve said as he shut Scott's door.

"What's wrong?" Travis and those damn sympathetic eyes would drive her nuts.

"I'm overwhelmed." She glided her fingers through her hair, tucking a stray hair behind her ear. "What's up with Steve? He seemed very cold."

"Steve's bark is worse than his bite," Travis said. "He's got big issues with women working in the field. Don't take it personally. I'm sure Scott's giving him a hard time as we speak." Travis, true to form, waited for her to enter their office first. "You're the new girl in town, don't be surprised if you get a lot of attention."

"I'm not fond of attention."

"Me neither." Travis propped his long legs on top of his desk and leaned back in his chair. Most of the men she'd known in her life had been cocky and arrogant, with no real reason to be that way. Travis, on the other hand, was confident and carried himself with an air of assurance, but he didn't act like he knew it all. Not bad to look at either. She tried not to stare, but that proved to be impossible.

"I'd like to ask some questions about those cases." She gave up trying not to gawk at him. She decided speaking to him would make it less obvious.

"Here." He dropped his feet to the floor and took some files from his desk.

"These are the official files. Look them over and then come tomorrow with questions or comments." He took a few steps, setting the folders in front of her before he sat on the edge of her desk.

She had to lean back in her chair. Looking up at

him, she had a bizarre urge to ruffle his perfect hair. She smiled.

"What?"

"Oh, nothing." She felt her cheeks flush.

"Would you like to get a bite to eat—partner?" He stood, knocking over a book. He tossed it back on her desk, then moved toward the window.

"Actually, I would, but I'd like to go home and change first. Meet you at my place in about an hour?"

"Works for me. I'll show you to your car." Travis waved her in front of him. "On second thought, I've got a better idea," he said from right behind her.

She could feel his warm breath on her neck. She liked it—a new feeling for her—but she didn't know where to file it, so she decided to try to ignore it.

"How about I cook you dinner?" He opened the standard four-door sedan she had been issued.

"You cook?"

He nodded. "This will give us a chance to look over those cases. Maybe you can catch something I missed."

She chuckled. "Another one of your tests?"

"I wish. This is the real thing." He jotted something down and handed her the piece of paper. "That's my address. You want directions?"

She looked down. She knew exactly where he lived, one block from the apartment she hoped to rent. "Give me an hour." She climbed in her new wheels and drove off.

Once she left the parking garage, she let out a big sigh. She had no idea she'd been holding her breath. What was she doing? She would be alone, with a man, in his apartment. "He's your partner. Get a grip," she reminded herself, worrying about what she should wear.

3

On the way home, Travis stopped at his favorite small mom and pop grocery store to pick up the necessary ingredients for dinner. He had decided on a shrimp and rice dish his grandmother used to make. Looking around the shop, he had half a mind to cancel. Having his female partner over for dinner didn't seem very professional.

He pulled a box of rice off the shelf, trying to convince himself that it was no different than having a male partner over for beer and a football game.

"Got a hot date?" Jimmy, the shop owner, asked.

"Nope." Travis smiled at Jimmy as he set his items on the register counter.

"Enough here for two?" Jimmy teased.

"Just showing off to my new partner." But why cook for her? If he'd been assigned a male partner, they'd probably end up at a hockey game, or more than likely, going their separate ways.

Jimmy started ringing up the items. Holding the shrimp in his hands, he said, "Must be a woman partner. I bet she's a real looker, too." He whistled, placing the items in a bag. He tossed in a few extra things like always. "The wife is going to love to hear about this one."

"Nothing to tell." Travis tossed him several bills, then held his hand up to refuse the change.

"Right. Tell me about the girl." Jimmy smiled, putting the money in the drawer. Half his teeth were missing, and his face looked like an old scrunched up piece of paper, but he had to be one of the most genuine people Travis had ever known.

"Not bad, but she's my partner. Strictly business."

"That's why you're cooking for her." Jimmy laughed. "One of these days the right woman is gonna sneak up on you."

Travis grabbed his bags. "I'm too difficult to live with." He waved and got in his truck. The right woman could come along, and Travis would still pass. Women, other than bed partners, were nothing but a distraction, and he wouldn't make that mistake again.

About a half hour later, Travis rolled up his sleeves and greased the wok. The oil popped and cracked as he added some seasoning and veggies, getting ready to drop in the shrimp.

The instant the shrimp started to change color, his

nose told him he was in heaven. *Almost as good as sex.* Shauna's face appeared in his mind. He shook his head and squelched his body's reaction.

Most of the women he dated were good-looking but forgettable. They were safe. See them a few times and then move on. He didn't really do one-night stands, but he didn't really do relationships anymore either.

He tossed the shrimp and veggies around in the wok. When he was satisfied they were done, he dumped them into the already cooked rice with his grandmother's secret sauce. He put the casserole dish in the oven and started to clean up.

His mind didn't stay lost in the task. It kept going back to his attractive new partner. Everything about her turned him on. Her intelligence intrigued him. She was beyond smart, and her instincts were natural, not to mention her vulnerability. He could sense she'd overcome something in her life, but he didn't have a clue as to what. Not that it mattered. He admired anyone who took adversity and used it to empower themselves. He'd like to believe that if Marie had survived, she would have done just that. He'd barely finished setting the table when the doorbell rang.

He glanced at his watch. Fifteen minutes early. He chuckled and opened the door, glad to know someone had listened to him. "Hi." He took her light coat and blinked as he caught her feminine scent. She smelled of fresh lilies or some spring flower. Actually, if he was being honest, she smelled of bottled sunshine, the perfect scent for a woman. The scent would prove to be his downfall if he wasn't careful.

"This place is great. I love the apartments on the upper level. I called on the one down the street." The excitement in her voice sent a certain body part of his climbing, a sensation that had to be stifled immediately.

"You get a chance to look at those case files?" He led her toward the kitchen.

"A little. What did you cook?" Her arm brushed against his bicep. She looked at him, then took a step back.

"Just a little something my grandmother taught me." He smiled. "Come on." Trying to lighten the obvious tension between the two of them, he nodded toward the kitchen.

"It smells great. Can I help?"

"Nah." He pulled the casserole dish from the oven.

"Wow. I'm impressed." She sat down while he piled food on her plate. "Can everyone in your family cook like this?" She closed her eyes, inhaling the rich aroma.

Holding the pot in one hand and the spatula in the other, he glared at her for a moment. What did she know about his family? He plopped some food on his plate, trying to shrug off his sudden distrust. "Promise not to laugh?" he asked, deciding her comment had to be a blanket statement. Everyone had a family.

"If it's funny, I'll laugh." She smiled at him.

"I'm the youngest boy and was always teased growing up." He sat down across from her and lifted his glass. "Cheers."

"Cheers."

Her pink lips touched the glass, and she took a sip of water. All he could think about was finding a way to get his lips on hers.

"Teased about what?" She licked them.

The table shook when he squirmed and tried to cross his legs, cutting off the circulation to a specific body part. Having dinner with his hot female partner was a really bad idea. "My brothers were jocks. And big. Actually, wide. They were known as the 'Double Mac Attack Brown Brothers.'" Travis winced at the memories of his two older, bigger, and much broader brothers. He had been a scrawny kid, but his choice in sports had been the clincher.

"Why not include you in the 'Mac Attack' thing?" She pursed her lips. "You're very...kind of...jock-like."

Travis laughed out loud. "It's the 'kind of' part that kept me from following in my older brothers' footsteps. Let's just say they're three times as wide as me and twice as strong."

"Whoa." She looked him over. "Still don't get it."

"They used to call me Travina." He found himself

laughing. He'd hated being called that as a kid, but now it was just plain funny.

"Excuse me?" She sipped her water. "As in a sissy? You? Never."

"I'd prefer to have been seen as that soft, sensitive kind of guy. You know, the one you want to bring home and cuddle with." He winked.

"Being a nice guy has nothing to do with masculinity. Why call you Travina for having the ability to cook and being sensitive?"

"Because they played football, hockey, and baseball, and I was on the gymnastics team. I was a little more limber than most of the girls, which caused me a lot of grief. Still does sometimes."

"I've seen some of those male gymnasts. You have to be pretty strong." She held up her arm, making a muscle.

Deciding it was time to change the subject, he took her fork and dug into a plump shrimp, lifting it to her mouth. "Here, try a bite." When she took the fork from his hands to feed herself, he scowled. What was he thinking making shrimp?

"Oh, God. You actually cooked this?" She stuffed another piece in her mouth. "Umm, my God."

The way she closed her eyes and rolled the food around in her mouth made a certain body part damn near climb right out of his pants. He forced himself to look at his own food and tried to think of anything other than the beautiful woman sitting across from him.

"Do your brothers cook?" Her voice was like hot lava rolling softly down a mountain, igniting a fire deep in his belly.

"Nope. They think it's for girls, like Travina."

"Your brothers must live in the dark ages, and I think you've got a great sense of humor." She smiled, waving her fork at him. "For the record, nothing about you is…well…hell, you're all man."

"Thanks. My parents kept telling me my time would come. My oldest brother is jealous as hell now. He thinks my job is too cool. My other brother lives in Lake Tahoe. Extreme skier of some kind. Still trying to find himself." Travis ate slowly, watching her. She devoured her meal like it was the Last Supper.

"You're all close?"

"Very. My oldest brother, Bill, lives in Lake George where I grew up. He's a high school biology teacher, married with three kids. Larry doesn't come home much, but we keep in touch. What about you?"

She put her fork down and looked blankly at him. Her blue eyes lost their spark.

"It's important for partners to know and understand each other." He smiled, leaning back in his chair.

"I don't see my family."

"I'm sorry." Travis wanted to reach out and touch her, comfort her. "Why not?" He knew he shouldn't ask, but the desire to know what made her tick outweighed his good senses.

She took a deep breath and glanced at the ceiling. "I didn't have the most pleasant childhood. When I took off for college, I never looked back."

Instinctively, he reached out and took her hand. Something in her voice told him there was a whole lot more to that story, but he wouldn't pry. Whatever it was, she was doing her best to move past it.

She pulled her hand away, took her napkin and wiped her mouth, then tossed it on her empty plate. "I don't dwell on it."

"You've obviously overcome a great deal to get where you are. You should be proud." He lifted the plates and took them to the sink.

"I am. It took me two extra years to get through college because I had to work to pay for it. I take responsibility for the outcome of my life." She stood next to him at the sink, washing a plate with vigorous strokes.

Gently, he took the plate from her hands. "I think it's clean."

"Oh." She rubbed her hands on her jeans, the kind that hugged the outline of her body. Right along with her not-so-loose T-shirt. "Most people want to feel sorry for me. I hate that."

"Hard to feel sorry for someone who's taken charge of their life. Besides, we all have our demons." He finished clearing the table to make room for the files. "Now, I want to know what you think about those cases." He desperately needed to get his mind away from her womanly shape.

"The only thing that comes up on all the cases is a mark on the back or the side of all the victims. In this case," she pushed a piece of paper in front of him, "it could've been caused by the barbed wire on the nearby fence. This second one, it seems obvious that the killer used a knife or some other sharp object." She tapped her finger at the picture of the girl found the day before she had arrived.

"This one looks like the tearing of the skin could've been from being dragged on the ground. This other case—the one you showed me last night—looks like he might have branded her or burned her." She never looked up. She kept her eyes and attention focused on the papers in front of her. There was a slight hitch in her voice.

When he looked at her strictly as an agent, he had to admire her concentration. "Not strong enough." He took in a deep breath. "Nothing really there to connect them by the scarring on their bodies."

She arched like a cat, rolling her fists in her back. "They're all runaways and in their teens."

"True, but we need more facts in the killer's MO, which really doesn't match, not just the victims." She looked across the table at him. "But you think it's the same guy."

The ability to speak one's mind had always been

something Travis admired in others; he liked the way she spoke her mind with him. "So do you." He stretched his legs out and leaned back, closing his eyes. A decision had to be made. These cases were open and the FBI was investigating them as a part of the Tri-City Joint Task Force; therefore, so was she. He had to wonder whether or not he should completely trust her. And what his boss would do to him if he found out. "Okay, maybe we should dig a little further," he said, opening his eyes.

"Where?" She sat up in her chair, excitement echoing in her voice.

He'd felt the same eagerness when he'd first started. "We start with this last case and work backward, but remember, this is on the bottom of our priority list. Any calls coming into the office come first, unless some other agency or law enforcement office asks us specifically to dig up these cases—got it?" Travis closed up the files and handed them to her.

She nodded. "It's late. We have a lot of work to do tomorrow. I'll walk you to your car." Travis slipped a jacket up to her shoulders doing his best to keep his fingers from lingering too long. Then without saying a word, she found her way down the stairs toward the street.

"Thanks for dinner," she said as she tried to unlock her car.

He took the keys from her shaking hands. "It was my pleasure."

"I want to mess up your hair." She covered her mouth. "Oh, God, I can't believe I just said that."

He winked. "Messing with my hair wouldn't be wise."

She took her keys, but when their fingers touched and eyes locked, he froze. A single strand of hair fell to her cheek. Gently, he brushed the silky lock behind her ear.

"Call me when you get back to your apartment." He took a step back, shoving his hands deep into his pockets. *Everything happens for a reason.* The words of his wise grandmother. If that were the case, then why did this woman walk into his life at this precise moment in time?

---

*T*he next week flew by in a haze of paperwork and training. Shauna barely had time to breathe. Or think about the way Travis's body decorated her office. By Friday morning, Shauna's eyes were dead tired, along with the rest of her aching muscles. Staring at all the lab sheets on her desk, she squirmed and stretched, trying to work out the kinks.

She picked up Jane Doe's file and briefly closed her eyes, remembering the moments of her life before she ran away.

One of her stepmother's friends suggested she try to model. Since she was so tall and thin, it made perfect sense. That's when she got the brilliant idea to run away. She took off to New York City the next week, and her life changed forever.

Holding the unrecognizable picture of herself, she glanced at Travis across the office. Honestly, she had nothing to hide. While the psychological tests she'd taken with the FBI revealed she'd been abused as a child, her responses indicated she'd dealt with her feelings and was a more than productive member of society. The tests actually showed a highly intellectual, compartmentalized, logical person who had adjusted to tragedy and risen above it.

Besides, from what she could gather, Travis seemed to know more about her assailant than she did. The only thing she'd be able to tell him would be the specifics of her rape. Even if Travis knew, she couldn't identify the killer. But she could recognize the killer's voice. Although she'd have to hear it first. Every man who opened his mouth around her, she listened to carefully. That voice was permanently imprinted on her brain.

She stuffed the picture in a file and looked at Travis again. He sat in his standard thinking position, feet on his desk, hands clasped behind his head, and it almost looked like he was reading something on the ceiling. He honestly thought Jane Doe held the key to unlocking this mystery.

Well, she didn't.

"Penny for your thoughts?" he said, not looking at her.

"Not much going on inside here. Honestly, I'm fried." She decided to try Travis's thinking position. She brushed the pleats in her pants, and in one quick motion, she lifted her legs and...

Crash! Thump.

"Humph." She gasped as she tumbled over backward. Thankfully she had chosen pants, because her legs flipped high over her head as her butt hit the floor.

"You okay?" Travis knelt down beside her, his hand extended before she had time to react.

She took it, giggling. "Just a bruised—uh, ego. You looked so comfortable." She rubbed her behind.

Leaning over her shoulder, he said, "Not enough padding back there."

She shot him a sideways glance. That was one of the few times he'd referenced her being a woman, besides the few awkward moments they'd shared when they locked gazes.

She had a difficult time fighting her attraction to him, and she suspected he had a similar problem. A warming sensation filled her body, but she forced herself to look away, hoping he didn't notice how she eyed him. Not very appropriate at work. He, on the other hand, had remained the consummate professional. Until now.

He tossed his hands wide. "Couldn't resist. You are really thin. Like a model."

She looked down at her chest and peeked in her shirt. "Certainly wouldn't make it as a lingerie model." She blinked and then looked up at the clock. It was almost five thirty.

Thank God the intercom buzzed before Travis had a chance to respond to her comment.

"What's up?" Travis hit a button on the phone.

"The president is on line two for you," the receptionist replied over the speakerphone.

Travis rolled his eyes.

"The president?" Shauna sat back down in her chair. *This could be interesting.*

He turned his back and picked up the receiver.

"Hi, Mom," he said, barely audibly.

Shauna bit her tongue. He put new meaning to the word 'contradiction.' Shauna couldn't find one thing about this man that she didn't like. His body was solid muscle, and his smile was the kiss of death for any woman. Her cheeks heated. Thank goodness he'd been looking the other way.

"I don't know, Mom. I'll have to ask." He turned. "My mom wants to know if you'd be willing to come up for dinner tomorrow night." He covered the mouthpiece. "She's invited every partner I've ever had up for dinner. Kind of a tradition. Not a big deal."

"Sure, why not?" She shrugged, feeling rough, sea-like sensations swish through her stomach.

"We'll be there," he said into the phone, then paused. "I love you, too. Bye, Mom."

"Does your mother have this effect on your brothers?" Shauna stood and collected everything she wanted to work on over the weekend and placed it in her briefcase, trying to ignore his playful stare.

"She has that effect on everyone. We all took up fishing. None of us really like it, but we get to be in control for just a few minutes."

A spark ran up her neck when his hand touched the small of her back. Not only was there a comfort level with him, but she also liked the way his gentle touch made her feel safe in his presence. She liked the way he smelled—like a man should smell—masculine, but sweet.

He dropped his hand. "Hey, Steve."

"Travis." Steve shook his head. "I hope he's been showing you around."

"Too busy doing our jobs," Travis said with real bite to his words, as if he were defending her honor or something. Had it been anyone else, she would have stepped in, but this was *her* partner who always treated her with equality, even when he was being a gentleman.

"Too bad. Please don't take this the wrong way, but I'll never understand why a pretty girl such as yourself would want a job like this. So many other things a girl could be doing."

"You're really—"

Shauna interjected, "I love what I'm doing. I'm good at it, and I would appreciate it if you would knock off those kinds of comments." It amazed her how willing Steve had been to show off his weaker, sexist side. Men had been fired for less.

Just then Jeff Wilcox stepped out of his office. "Hey." He slapped Travis on the back. "Got any plans tonight, Shauna? I'd love to show you around...unless Travis already beat me to the punch. Or maybe Steve, here." He elbowed Travis in the side.

"Buzz off, Wilcox," Steve said in an almost protective tone. The two men seemed like opposites, except they both had issues with women, although Steve didn't seem like a player, just insanely old school. Jeff, on the other hand, had the attitude of a womanizer. The way he slinked around the office, always checking himself out every time he passed a mirror, drove her nuts. He wasn't bad-looking with his short, dark hair and constant five o'clock shadow, but dating material? Never.

"Hey, just trying to be social," Jeff said. "So, who wants to go have a drink?"

"Not this time. I grew up near here and have a lot of friends I'd like to catch up with," Shauna added, hoping everyone would just go away.

"Not tonight." Steve frowned and then ducked into his office.

"Bummer. Guess I'm on my own. Another time?"

Jeff whistled some tune, and with a funky spring in his step, sauntered out of the building.

"I know that song." Shauna rubbed her temples. "What was he whistling?"

"I have no idea," Travis said. "Do you want to get a drink?"

The darkness of the parking garage sent a familiar fear rippling through her mind. She stepped closer to Travis, trying to find that sense of comfort he'd been known to give her by just being near.

"I probably shouldn't be going with you tomorrow. I don't need office gossip, and we're digging in places that could get you in a whole heap of trouble. Just because the Troy and Albany police departments asked us to look into possible connections, doesn't mean Scott's going to give you free reign. I, on the other hand, get to play dumb."

"Thanks for the reminder, but you can't pull off the newbie act. You're too damn smart." He opened her car door for her and looked around. "And if I dare say it, too damned beautiful."

She tried to avoid his heavenly blue eyes, but it was too late. Another awkward moment. She couldn't deny there were sparks. And she knew he couldn't either.

"I'll pick you up at nine."

"In the morning?" she questioned.

"You don't want to make me disappoint my

mother, do you?" His smile drew slowly across his face.

Damn him. She forced her eyes closed and shook her head. "I'll be ready." She slipped into the driver's seat, letting him close the door for her. "Thanks."

"For what?"

"Seeing me as an intelligent person before a pretty face."

"Intelligent only scratches the surface. The pretty part, well, let's just say that I don't think I've had a partner who was better looking than me." He winked. "Until now."

If she were any other woman, she would have gotten out of the car, ruffled his hair, and kissed his face off. But she was Shauna Morgan, and any physical relationship with this man would be disastrous.

She waved and hit the gas. Travis was a dangerous man. He actually made her want to try a relationship again. Bad idea. Not only could they both lose their jobs if anything happened, but he wasn't going to be too happy when he found out who she really was.

4

The following morning Travis stepped out of his apartment and into the sunlight. The birds sang, and the smell of lilacs filtered through his nose. Biting back a sneeze, he adjusted his dark sunglasses and got into his truck. No matter how hard he tried, he couldn't ignore the feeling his new partner was hiding something.

Typically, going home for a visit didn't give him a sense of dread, but today he felt different. The piercing sun stung his eyes as he headed east toward Shauna's apartment. He'd always been close to his family, and they knew all about his theories on who'd killed his sister. So did everyone in the office. It wasn't like he kept it a secret, and he was sure someone would have warned her about his little 'obsession' as Scott called it.

The truck jumped forward as he slapped the

steering wheel. Shauna had to have known about his sister. He pulled into the parking lot in front of the lobby doors. He slammed the door shut, entered the lobby, and made his way down the torn-up hallway. It seemed the residence inn had started renovations.

This new case gave him cause to dig. The same thing any good agent would do, especially when the police had no leads and suspected the girl had been kidnapped, making that particular case the FBI's business. None of that explained Shauna's apparent secretiveness. He'd given her all the open case files. She was smarter than most, and with access to all the FBI files, which he knew she spent hours working on, there was no way she would have missed the connection. His sister had been murdered; it was obvious she knew. So why not say something?

Why did she have such passion for these cases in the first place? It wasn't like it was personal for her, like it was for him. There had to be a reason she was so interested in this particular murderer.

A sharp pain rippled from his knuckles to his wrists as he pounded on the door.

"Coming." The wood that separated them muffled her voice.

"Hi," she said, opening the door, but he turned, looking back down the hallway toward the lobby.

The smell of warm peaches and cream filled his nostrils. He glanced over his shoulder, catching her slight smile as she closed the door.

"Let's go," he said, trying not to notice her legs. He'd seen them before, but never completely uncovered.

After opening the door for her, he got in his pickup and headed for the Northway. He forced his thoughts from the beautiful woman sitting beside him and made himself think of a partner —partner, *not* woman. The one who he had begun to think had a hidden agenda. "So why haven't you made any comments about my sister?" He glanced at her as he navigated through traffic.

"I figured you didn't want to talk about it. I wondered…when I got this assignment…if she might be related to you."

Her normal confident poise faltered a bit. He took her inability to open up as sign of mistrust. "You knew before you came here?" Long silence followed. She stared out the window. She'd occasionally twirl her fingers through her hair.

"I'd seen the name and read some of the paperwork while at Quantico doing case studies."

"Why didn't you say anything?"

"You already asked that, and I answered."

"I want to hear your answer again," he said.

"I didn't want to pry. If you wanted to talk about it, I figured you would."

"What do you know about my sister?" Sitting at a stoplight, he turned and narrowed his eyes.

"I picked her case in one of my courses. I had to try to poke holes in the conviction."

"Why Marie's case?"

"My paper was on Matt Williams. I tried to prove that he couldn't have killed Marie."

The truck jerked forward. "What about Jane Doe? What about the other girls' cases he was convicted of? You include them?"

"The paper included all convictions." She turned and looked at him. "The D.A. didn't bring up charges regarding Jane Doe, so I had to leave her out of it."

"Care to share your findings?"

"I couldn't find anything that compelling. I got a C on the stupid paper, but I can give you a copy if you want."

"Why not bring it up when you were first assigned to work with me?" He pulled into his parents' driveway and turned to her. "If you did your research, you had to know who I was." He gripped the steering wheel tightly.

"I knew," she said. "Just trying to be respectful."

"Right." He blinked, staring at the tree in the front yard. "Are you here to keep an eye on me? Did the FBI put you in my office to keep me in line?"

"Not that I know of."

Her tone indicated she was being truthful, but he had reservations. Scott had been relatively cool about the off-duty work Travis did with regard to his sister's case file, but Scott had also warned Travis on numerous occasions to keep the digging to a minimum because someday Travis would piss off the wrong agent. "Do you believe Williams did it?"

"It doesn't matter what I believe." She sighed. "They convicted someone, case closed. Besides, he was a badass and guilty of a lot of other shit."

He couldn't argue with that, but his instincts told him she had just fed him a line. Before he told her everything, he had to find out what she wasn't telling him.

---

*S*hauna waited for Travis to open the door for her. He always treated her with the utmost respect. Her opinions mattered, and he asked for them constantly, but when he took her hand in his, she couldn't deny the electricity his touch created. No matter how badly she wanted to.

A noise coming from the house caught her attention, thankfully grounding the electric pulses.

The door to a modest, yet beautifully kept house closed, and a little girl of maybe six or seven skipped down the flower-lined walkway. Her long, auburn locks bounced every time her feet hit the ground.

"Uncle Trav!" The little girl smiled wide.

"Hey, squirt."

She leapt at Travis.

"Who's the girl?" The young girl giggled, eyeing Shauna.

"This is my partner, Shauna. Shauna, this is Kamy." He smiled proudly as he tickled Kamy's belly.

"Hi, Kamy," Shauna said, reaching out to brush back a piece of the girl's hair, but yanked her hand back.

"You're an agent?" Kamy said with wide eyes.

Shauna nodded, stuffing her hands in her pockets.

"Oh, way too cool."

Travis put Kamy down, and she went running back toward the house, yelling to her parents. "She's pretty energetic."

Shauna felt a warm tingle begin at the base of her back and spread up her spine and into her muscles. Slight pressure from his hand eased the growing discomfort as they made their way up the stone walkway toward the house. Of all the places she thought she might end up, Marie's home wasn't one of them.

"Well, lookie what the cat dragged in." A very broad, muscular man opened the front door.

He looked like a hundred-year-old tree trunk. She wanted to poke him to see if he was just as solid. While the man in the door looked very much like Travis, their builds couldn't be more different. Travis was about two inches taller, but nowhere near as broad. Not even close.

"Hey, bro. Where's everyone?" Travis slapped his

brother's back and motioned to Shauna to enter the house.

"Dad took Adam fishing, and Jessica's still in bed. Teenagers. I can't take it." Travis's brother shook his head. "She's even got a boyfriend who's coming for dinner."

"You had a girlfriend at that age," Travis teased.

"I remember all too well what I was thinking and trying when I was fourteen." Chuckling and rolling his eyes, the older man glanced at Shauna, then back at Travis. "Oh, man. Mom would have your head right now."

"Yeah, well, you're not Mom. Shauna, this is my much older brother, Bill. Bill, my new partner, Shauna."

"Nice to meet you," Shauna said with shaky voice. She had always hoped for the opportunity to meet with Travis and discuss his sister's case on a professional level but had never thought she'd meet Marie's family.

"The pleasure's all mine." Bill took her hand and shook it firmly.

Shauna glanced around what she assumed was the family room, but only because it felt homey. Warm-colored couches graced the hardwood floors. Pictures of children playing, swimming, and being kids lined the walls. This was a room where people gathered just to be together.

"Travis?" A beautiful woman entered the family

room. Her grace and soft smile filled the space with warm fuzzies, actually calming Shauna's stomach.

"Hi, Mom."

Shauna had to blink. His mother had to be the most beautiful woman she had ever seen. And the most poised. She stood tall and proud. Her dark hair was pulled back away from her angelic face. Her crisp-blue eyes were soft and welcoming. A strong feeling of understanding overcame Shauna, and she immediately felt a connection to his mother.

"Are you going to introduce me? Or do I need to give you a lesson in manners?" She ruffled Travis's hair.

"Mom, this is my new partner, Shauna Morgan. Shauna, meet the president." He ran his hands through his thick, dark hair.

"Get it right. It's a dictatorship in this household. Hi, Shauna. Please, call me Rita."

Shauna smiled, stifling a little giggle. She'd wanted to run her hands through his gorgeous hair and mess it up since she'd met him. "I'm sorry," she said, after a chuckle escaped her lips.

"Don't be, honey. Here, I'll do it again." Rita went for Travis's hair.

"Mother, please."

"Oh, don't 'Mother, please' me." Rita's eyes illuminated the room. "Is Jessica awake? And where's Kim?" Rita tugged both of her sons' ears. Both gave the same playful grimace.

Shauna's body trembled on the inside as she took a deep breath. A warm apple and cinnamon smell filled her nostrils, and a sense of love filled her heart. Not something she was used to. Her home had consisted of moldy dishes and the back of her father's hand across her cheek. Instinctively, she rubbed her face.

"Dad! Why do I have to get up? It's the freaking weekend," a voice echoed from the hall.

"Watch that tongue of yours, young lady." Rita glared at the teenager slinking down the dim hallway.

"Sorry, Grandma, but it's Saturday." The young girl kept her face to the floor as she pushed back her dark, shoulder-length hair.

"Jessica, your uncle's here." Rita's tone softened.

"Hey, Uncle Trav. Who's the chick?" the young girl asked. She wore a pair of worn flannel pajama bottoms rolled down at the waist, and a camisole that hid nothing.

When Jessica lifted her head, Shauna's heart skipped. Jessica could have been Marie's twin. Shauna forced herself to gaze toward the other people in the room.

"Get some clothes on," Bill barked.

"That's funny coming from you, Dad. Ya know he walks around the house naked all the time. It's gross. You datin' my uncle?" Her eyes were gold in color… and innocent. So innocent.

"I'm Shauna, his partner."

"FBI?" Jessica pursed her lips, then rolled her eyes just as her father had done. "Grandma, you said he was bringing up a girl, not his partner. I think there's a difference."

Rita stiffened her back. "None of you gave me a chance to finish my sentence."

"Good one, Mother," Travis said before Rita pushed out her hand.

"Okay, enough of this." Rita waved her arms. "We all have things to do this morning. So let's get to it." She clapped her hands twice, then scurried off.

"Sorry about that." Travis took Shauna by the arm and led her though the house to a porch overlooking the lake.

"No girlfriend, huh?" Shauna's stomach swished in excitement. He had told her that the more they knew about each other, the better their working partnership would be. Well, she planned on milking that one to find out all she could about him.

"Nope." A genuine smile appeared across his face.

"Gay?" She had to bite the inside of her cheek to keep herself from laughing. The contorted look on his face was priceless.

"Excuse me?" He coughed, glaring at her.

She giggled. "Sorry, but a guy like you?" She looked him over. "Gorgeous, sexy as hell, and a gentleman to boot; I can't imagine why you haven't landed yourself a girl, unless of course you lean to the other side, if you know what I mean."

"I'm picky." He scowled. "I'm not gay."

"I know that." She shook her head. "It was a joke."

"Never joke about a man's...manhood." He pushed open a sliding glass door and nudged her outside.

"Wow." Shauna closed her eyes and inhaled sharply. The crisp lake scent made her dizzy. She gripped his arm as she opened her eyes. "This is breathtaking." She looked out over the tree-lined shore. The house was nestled on a slight incline. Her nose filled with fresh spring floral scents, and the water rippled in the sun's dancing reflection.

"I forget how spoiled I was sometimes."

"You're very lucky." She forced herself to look at the lake. When he squeezed her shoulder, a small shudder shot down her spine.

"Come on." Taking her by the elbow, he guided her down the rocky staircase-like path to the dock. "I want to go for a boat ride."

"Thought we had things to do?" She looked down at the path, concentrating on putting one foot in front of the other. Her heart fluttered in anticipation. But of what?

"My job is to entertain you." He gave her a very sexy grin.

"Oh." Shauna followed him toward the dock. "How many boats do you have?" she asked, searching for small talk. She felt uncomfortable because she felt so at ease with him.

"My parents have two: the fishing boat—it isn't here right now—and that sailboat." He nodded to a relatively large boat moored in front of the dock. "This is Bill's boat. He lives over there." The gentle touch of his hand on her shoulder made her quiver. His lips were inches from her cheek as he leaned over and pointed across the bay. "The one two doors down from the marina. My mom likes it when they spend the night. So they humor her now and again."

"That's nice," she said, pulling away from him.

He licked his lips as his eyes diverted to her mouth. "Take my hand," he said softly.

Looking down at his outstretched hand, she placed hers in his and closed her eyes for a moment. She shouldn't feel like this. Not with him.

"Watch your step."

The old-fashioned wooden boat tipped slightly when she stepped on the side. "I love these old boats." She sat down next to the driver's seat.

Travis untied the boat and jumped in, sending it rocking from side to side. "Sorry." He smiled, settling himself down in the driver's seat, turning the key. He idled away from shore, then pushed down on something, causing the boat to pick up speed. Her hair brushed across her face. "This is incredible."

"If it wasn't such a commute, I might consider living up here someday."

A large tour boat tooted its horn as it drove by.

"I worked on that ship for two summers."

"Really?" She smiled, looking at the large floating tour bus. "Doing what?"

"Deckhand."

"What's that?" She glanced at him as he slowed the boat.

"I got to untie her, then tie her up." He leaned forward as if to share a secret. "I even got to scrub the deck and galley."

"Sounds like—whoa." The boat lurched up and smacked down against the water, sending her into his lap.

"Hello," he said as they locked gazes.

Her body trembled as he slowed the boat, then shut off the engine. "Oops." The keys dropped from his fumbling fingers. He drew her closer, tracing her jawline with his finger. "I think we might have a problem," he mused.

A flock of seagulls squawked from above, but that didn't break her intense gaze with his. Try as she might, she couldn't turn away. Or get off his lap.

His fingers were tangled in her hair, making her body scream for the kind of human contact she'd been avoiding most of her life. She tried to utter something but couldn't. The desire to be wanted by this man was greater than her good senses—the consequences be damned.

His hand cupped the back of her head, pulling at her hair with tender care. When his soft, warm lips brushed hers, she moaned. The electricity that flowed between them shocked and frightened her. She'd never felt a kiss so powerful, and she'd never allowed herself to be out of control.

At the sound of a horn, she jerked back, opening her eyes wide. The boat rocked from waves of other boats sloshing the water, but her body trembled from feelings she didn't understand. It wasn't like she'd never been with a man before. She'd had other relationships, a few lovers, and had been through counseling. She'd long since moved past being raped. But somehow those experiences had been forgettable. In his arms, she felt like she belonged.

"Smartass." He waved to some guy in a boat as it sped by, then slowed. "Sorry about that."

She coughed.

"Are you okay?"

The soft, gentle tone of his words made her want to scream, *No! I'm not okay! You drive me nuts, and I'm the woman you've been searching for!* She nodded. "Just caught off guard."

"By the kiss? My idiot friend? Or the fact that I'm far from gay?" He chuckled.

She didn't have time to respond. His idiot friend just pulled up. While Travis was distracted, she took the time to pull herself together and shift as far from him as she could.

"Shauna, this is Jake Hanson. Jake, this Shauna Morgan."

"Nice to meet you," Jake said.

"Likewise."

"How are things going?" Jake asked.

"The same," Travis said.

"Make any connections?"

"Nope. What about you?"

"Nothing concrete, but I'll let you know what I find out." Jake said. "How long are you here for?"

"Just the day."

"Too bad. Lana would have loved to see you. Not to mention meet your new partner." Jake smiled. "Besides, you haven't seen the twins yet. Cutest little buggers you've ever seen. I really outdid myself this time." Jake grinned.

Travis laughed. "And Lana had nothing to do with it."

"She's got Katie." Jake smiled.

"Katie's a daddy's girl." Travis shook his head. "I doubt I'll get over this trip, but I do need to pick your brain sometime."

"Anytime." Jake waved and buzzed off.

Shauna looked the other way. That kiss still lingered on her lips, and she didn't like it. To be honest, she didn't like the fact that she liked it. She couldn't afford to be distracted. Finding out what Travis knew and nailing her attacker were the only things she should be thinking about.

*T*ravis pulled the boat into the slip with ease, but he'd mentally given himself a good tongue-lashing for trying to kiss Shauna. Not one of his most brilliant moments. Regardless of the sparks that had been flying, kissing her was truly his kiss of death.

The rest of the day he let her get overtaken by his family, just so he could stay away. Every time he got near her, he forgot why he was with her in the first place. He liked women, but most didn't affect him to the point of distraction.

Sitting out on the front porch, legs stretched up on the railing, Travis held his sister's picture in one hand and a soda in the other. There were moments he missed her so much it hurt, like now.

"Jessica looks a lot like her," Shauna said, pulling up a chair.

"Jesus." His feet hit the floor with a thud. "You shouldn't sneak up on armed men."

She took the picture from him. "Is Jessica like Marie at all?"

"Marie was very stubborn, like my brother Larry. Bill and I always tried to just get along. Those two were rebels without causes. Jessica is kind of in between. She acts all tough on the outside, but I suspect she's just like her father."

"A big teddy bear on the inside." Shauna smiled.

"He's married." Travis smiled back. She had a way of breaking down his defenses and making him feel like he could tell her anything.

"Married, but adorable."

"We try not to mention the similarities too much. Bill says the whole thing seems to really bother Jessica."

Shauna pointed her face in the direction of the sun, and Travis took advantage. He let his gaze enjoy her creamy-looking skin and her touchable curves. But he kept his hands to himself.

"Why'd she run away?"

"There are times I'm not sure she did run away." He stretched his arms out to the side, tilting his head. "She'd told my parents she was staying after school with some friends and she'd take the late bus home. She wasn't on that bus, and it was three days before they found her."

"I'm really sorry." Her gentle touch sent a feeling of understanding through his skin to his heart. He glanced at her face and studied her deep expression. "What are you thinking?" He touched her knee.

The sparkle in her eyes from the reflection of the sun off the crystal-blue lake made it difficult for him to focus on anything but her.

"If you look at the open cases, it looks like we have two killers. One who rapes, kills, and just dumps the bodies in the woods," she said.

"The others are cleaned, as if he is trying to get rid of any traces of rape. Or maybe cleanse their souls." He scooted to the edge of his seat, riveted by her instincts.

"The same killer wouldn't change his MO," she commented, pausing, biting her thumbnail. "But what if it everything hinges on whether or not the girls were virgins?"

"Not easy for a dead girl to tell us her past sexual history."

"I take it you've already thought of that?"

He'd never seen her bite her nails before. Something about this conversation made her nervous, which in turn made him nervous because she was the most confident woman…no, FBI agent he'd ever met. "I once presented it to one of the other agents when I first started. I was informed that it would have to be perceived virginity, since it is possible for the hymen to be broken other ways."

"Perceived virginity could be the key though." With a shaking hand, she tucked a piece of hair behind her ear.

"What's going on inside there?" He tapped her forehead, hoping she'd open up to him. She had a theory, or an idea, and he wanted her to share it.

"What if we approach this as two different killers? At least, that's how we present it to the task force. I think there's enough to link the two hotel cases together."

Travis held up his hand. "Too many years between them."

"Don't you see?" Her voice cracked.

"We need a bigger connection before we present

this to make it more than a file we're continuing to aid the police on. You are onto something, though; we just need to dig a little deeper, like find Jane Doe."

"Maybe she doesn't want to be found," his mother said, standing directly behind him and breathing down his neck. "Maybe she wants to forget and move on with her life. Like you should."

Avoiding his mother's painful stare, he said, "I can't get over it, and neither can you." He clenched his fists.

"I'll always miss my Marie. If I could've changed places with her, I would have, but I'm not going to let some psycho dictate what I do. She was my only daughter." A tear dripped down his mother's cheek. "If I could bring her back, I would."

"Putting the jerk behind bars will certainly make me feel better." He looked out over the lake, trying to find some calming aspect of his surroundings.

"They already put one behind bars."

"The wrong man, Mother." The small plastic table knocked over as he leapt to his feet, sending his soda can spraying down the stone path.

"Well, he was guilty of something and belongs in prison."

"So does the man who raped and killed Marie," Travis said.

His mother let out a long, slow breath. "Are you prepared to bring an innocent young girl into this? She may not believe they caught the wrong guy. Do you want to ruin her sense of security? Don't you think she's been through enough?"

"If that monster is still out there, she'll never be safe." The wood railing shook with his trembling hands. He struggled to keep his anger from igniting an all-out war of words. "I just want to protect her," he said behind a clenched jaw.

"If she believed he was still out there, don't you think she'd come forward?"

"Not if she's smart."

"Oh, that's right. She'd stay hidden because she knows her attacker is out there," his mother said. "I loved Marie as much as you did, but you have to move forward. Live your life, don't live in her memory."

"I don't want to argue."

"Then drop it. I don't think you see what you're doing to this family. Now if you would excuse me," she said softly and went back into the house.

"Your mother's right," Shauna said.

Travis's pulse increased. "What the hell does that mean?"

"I might be out of line, but your world seems too wrapped up in the past."

"One, you're out of line. Two, didn't you just think we should present all this to the task force?"

"Yes, but not under the pretense of looking for your sister's killer. We're looking for the man who raped and murdered those girls. Even if they are one in the same, that is immaterial, as is Jane Doe."

"But she might be able to help."

Shauna stood and faced him. "While you say you want to protect Jane Doe, just talking to her could bring her out in the open, reveal her identity. If what we believe is true, if this is the same guy, and if he finds out who she is—" Shauna blinked, "—then he'll kill her. Can you live with that? Because I know I can't."

"I doubt he knows who she is, or he would have gone after the one person who could nail his ass. What happened to those instincts of yours?"

"Call these womanly instincts, but I doubt Jane Doe wants to be identified." Something flickered behind her eyes. "Besides, what would the bureau do with us if we got caught trying to find a woman's rapist who technically has been sitting in prison for years? We need to focus on the caseload we have. The victims we can tie to *a* killer, not the one that haunts you."

"Jane Doe holds the key to our caseload. We need to find her. And we can do it on our own time." Travis turned and entered the house. The one time he thought he had someone in his corner, thinking his way, she turns on him. Figures.

Well, he would make sure she came around to his way of thinking; she had to. She was too damn smart not to.

5

S hauna lingered on the porch, trying to enjoy the sunset against the shimmer of the crystal-clear lake. A few boats hummed along the shoreline like a picture on a postcard. But there was nothing picture-perfect about this situation. She feared her job would be on the line if any of her superiors knew she was 'The Jane Doe' in a case that involved her partner's dead sister.

A loud shriek followed by a splash and a roar of laugher brought her attention to two teenagers frolicking about in the water. Letting out a huge sigh, she closed her eyes and tried to remember the happy times in her childhood. But there were none.

"Hi." Kamy's squeaky little voice danced in her ears.

"Hi." Shauna smiled as the little girl climbed up on her legs. The brushing of Kamy's soft skin felt warm against Shauna's cold memories. This child had the world at her hands and love in her heart.

"Mommy says you're pretty. I do, too," Kamy said as she settled into Shauna's lap, smelling like peaches.

"I think you're much prettier than me." Shauna batted Kamy's nose.

"There you are." Kim slipped through the patio door. "You can't just walk off like that, baby."

"I'm not a baby!" Kamy pouted.

"You're my baby. I hope she wasn't bothering you." Kim patted the girls head.

"She's no bother. I enjoy her company," Shauna said.

"She is full of sweetness, that's for sure." Kim lifted Kamy into her arms and gave her a big smooch on the cheek. "Let's go get cleaned up for dinner."

Shauna stood and stared out over the water, concentrating on the soft roll of the water crashing against the shore, instead of the heartache she felt deep in her soul.

"I'm sorry for my outburst." Rita appeared at her side.

"Don't apologize." Shauna looked into the same intense eyes Travis had and swallowed.

"Travis is a very passionate man." Rita rounded her shoulders. "He's also very stubborn."

"I've noticed."

"May I ask you a question?" Rita touched Shauna's hands. She nodded, trying not to tremble.

How could she stand here, look this woman in the eye, and not tell her?

Because to tell her would probably destroy her.

"Do you think Jane Doe could help?"

Shauna broke out in a cold sweat, and she was sure her face drained of all color. "I'm sure if Jane Doe knew anything, she'd find a way to help." On some level, Shauna wanted to scream, *I'm right here.* But what good would that do? She couldn't ease their pain or deliver that bastard to them. "Truthfully, I don't know. Your daughter's case is officially closed, and all the reports indicate that Jane Doe was attacked by the same man, although that was never proven."

"I know Travis believes other innocent girls have died, but I wonder if simply talking to Jane Doe would ease his pain."

It would probably only add to it, which was why Shauna had to keep her identity a secret. She set this lie in motion, now she had to live with it. "I'm not sure. However, I do believe we need to focus his attention on the here and now cases, especially those that are similar."

"Do you believe the authorities convicted the right man?"

Not an easy question to answer without giving herself away. "I really don't know. For now, I think Travis has too much on his mind, and it's blending with his past. He's a very determined man."

"Yes, he is," Rita smiled. "When the cops first picked up Williams for my daughter's murder, I was relieved. I felt as though I had some kind of closure, but with Travis's thoughts and convictions, I have to wonder. He's very smart and very good at what he does."

"Yes, he is."

"Sometimes I think we're all just nuts," Rita said.

"I don't think any of us are nuts." Shauna fought the tears that begged to run down her cheeks. The need to be strong for this family outweighed her personal agony.

Rita pulled Shauna into the kitchen with her. "Enough of this serious stuff." Rita placed a cutting board in front of Shauna. "You get to slice the cucumbers."

"I think I can handle that."

Rita put her hands on her hips. "So, tell me. Is my son behaving himself?"

"Oh, yeah. Always the gentleman," Shauna said.

"He was the easiest of the boys to train. I told him it was his job to teach Marie how to be a lady. I think he took it a little too seriously." Rita held a locket that dangled from her neck, gave it a quick kiss, and smiled at Shauna.

"What else can I do?" Shauna asked, praying that it didn't consist of actually cooking anything.

"I think we're all set. John's got the steaks on the

grill, so just take this salad to the table." Rita handed a bowl to her.

"I can handle that."

"Are agents allowed to date each other?" Rita opened the door to the dining room with a slight grin.

"I think it's highly frowned upon," Shauna said between gasping breaths, and then came face-to-face with most of the Brown family.

While the dining room seemed spacious, she felt closed in. She sat in her chair, hoping no one really noticed her. Being a part of a normal family was not something she knew anything about.

"I'm told you grew up in Saratoga," John, Travis's father, said to her over the noise of the kids.

She nodded, trying to avoid getting pulled into the conversation. If she remained quiet, she thought they'd continue with their own family discussions, letting her blend in with the furniture.

"Do you have a lot of family there?" Rita asked. Her smile gave Shauna a sense of warmness, but it was the sensitive look in Rita's eyes that gave her the courage to answer.

"My dad lives there, but we're not close."

"That's sad," Jessica said. "My dad's a pain, but I think I'll keep him." She batted her eyelashes at her father.

"Jess, I said no." Bill gave his daughter a pointed glare.

"Mr. Brown?" Kirk, Jessica's boyfriend, piped in.

"Would it make a difference that my mother is one of the chaperones?"

"It might. Would she be driving you back and forth?" Bill cocked his head.

"Yep, I mean…yes, sir." The young boy shot upright in his chair.

Shauna watched as her heart filled with a mixture of emotions that she didn't know where to file. "What are we talking about?" She placed her elbows on the table, resting her chin in her hands.

"A dance! Kirk asked me to a dance with his church on the *Minnie Ha Ha*, a cruise boat that circles around the bay near the village," Jessica answered. Excitement danced in her soft-gold eyes.

"I've never been to a dance, or on the *Minnie Ha Ha*," Shauna said.

"What about the prom? I can't believe you didn't go to your prom," Travis said, placing his fork on his plate.

She looked around the room, feeling all eyes on her. Why did the prom mean so much to some people anyway? "Not a big deal." She shrugged.

"I won't believe that no one asked you," Kim said, looking shocked.

"I wasn't really into it," Shauna replied.

"Nuh-uh, no way. Someone had to ask you. You are way too hot—um, I mean pretty," Kirk said, while his face turned three shades of red.

"Thanks." Shauna smiled. "But no one asked, and I wasn't interested."

"Girls ask boys to dances all the time," Jessica added, looking into her plate.

"Not a lady." Rita patted Jessica, who sat up straighter.

"Ladies can ask," Kim added, with squinted eyes. "We don't live in the dark ages anymore."

"I still don't think young girls should be so forward." Rita gave the squint back, but she smiled playfully.

"And that's why Grandma asked me to the formal, long before we started going steady."

"I most certainly did not." Rita narrowed her eyes.

Out of the blue, Shauna wanted more than what she'd had most of her life. Now that she had her dream career, it seemed she wanted more. She didn't want to feel alone anymore, except until now, she hadn't realized she felt lonely. Her therapist used to argue with her about her inability to form meaningful relationships. Of course, Shauna had always replied that she got enough meaning out of her relationships with her fellow agents in training.

"She also told me that she might say yes if I asked her to marry me." John stood, helping Rita clear the table.

Shauna watched everyone roll their eyes, including Travis.

"How can you tell such fibs?" Rita swatted her husband's arm. "I mean, really. I would never."

John whispered something in Rita's ear.

She giggled.

A few minutes later, Shauna found herself alone in the large family room. She took in a deep breath, taking in all the scents from dinner and dessert, and realizing she'd never smelled anything so wonderful in her life. Being here with his family made her heart flutter, skipping beats, knowing this was how life should be.

However, her life could never be like this.

Even if she did find her attacker, she'd never have this. There would always be another attacker. Another rapist to catch. Another murder to solve. Another victim to help.

She held up a picture of Marie and Travis. Tears fought to break free, but she wouldn't let them drop. She'd get through this without falling apart. Her life depended upon it.

---

*T*ravis watched Shauna interact with his family with a degree of sadness. She seemed withdrawn, and he wondered how much of her life had been spent having to fight. No one should be alone in the world. Then again, the last few years he'd gotten used to being by himself. However, no matter how distant he got, he could always come home. Funny how someone can make you rethink things.

Travis followed Bill down to the dock. The boat needed to be cleaned and battened down for the night. Somehow, no matter who used the fishing boat, Travis and Bill always had to take care of it.

"You're in big trouble, little brother," Bill said as he gathered up the fishing tackle.

"What are you babbling about?" As if Travis didn't know. When it came to women, he'd always been such an easy read. Not a single crush went by unnoticed, or without mega family teasing.

"That's one damn good-looking woman."

"She's smart, too." Travis hooked his finger with a fishing lure. "Shit." The blood dripped to the dock.

"Oh, big trouble. Especially since Mom is on the prowl again. She wanted me to fix you up with the new gym teacher." Bill tossed him a bucket. "I told Mom she was gay."

"At least Mom doesn't think I'm gay." Travis smirked.

"Huh?" Bill stopped and stared at Travis.

"Never mind."

"Yeah, well...Mom has a point."

"Mom doesn't know everything," Travis said.

"She won't let up." Bill tossed something at Travis but missed. "She'll hound you until she finds you the perfect woman."

"Just like she did for you?" Travis shot some extra fish guts at him.

"Kim and I picked each other."

"After Mom did everything in her power to get the two of you together."

"She sure as hell didn't get Kim pregnant. I did that all on my own." Bill flicked his wet hands at Travis with a smug grin.

"And we're proud of this fact?" Travis took a step closer.

"As a matter of fact, I am. Mother was a little disappointed that it happened before we got married, but it got me to the altar, didn't it?"

Travis smiled. There was no place for Bill to go but the lake. "If memory serves me correctly, Kim didn't want much to do with you." He stood inches from Bill. "How'd you manage to get her to sleep with you anyway?"

"The same way you'll end up in bed with your partner. Hot animal attraction."

That did it. Travis shoved.

Bill started to fall backward, waving at Travis.

"Crap." He blinked as Bill yanked on the rope tangled in Travis's feet, and they both went…

Splash.

"Real mature," Kim said as she made her way onto the dock. "You'd think two grown men could take care of one chore without ending up in the lake."

"Come here and help me, hon." Bill reached his arm out.

"Not on your life, *hon*. Hurry it up. We have to get the boyfriend home." She held out a towel.

"Where's my towel?" Travis asked.

"Mom told me to collect mine. Shauna was told to collect hers. I think Mom is explaining the birds and the bees to her."

Bill laughed.

"Jerk." Travis dunked him and then heaved himself up on the dock. "Damn it." He fell backward when Bill pulled him.

"My wife, my towel. Get your own, on both accounts." Bill took his towel and kissed his wife.

"So, he got the hots for her or what?" Kim glanced over her shoulder.

"That doesn't cover what he's got for her. Let's go embarrass the heck out of our daughter."

Travis lingered in the water, waiting. His mother would make Shauna come down eventually.

Just as he was about to give up hope, he saw her figure slink down the stairs in the moonlight. Oh yeah, hot didn't cover it, but he was going to have to hide his reaction to it. On a regular basis for the next two years. Yep, right now his job sucked.

"Your mother seems to think you're in need of a towel." Shauna stood near the edge of the dock, not looking too pleased about the situation.

Knowing he had other plans, he smiled to himself.

"Did you bring two?" The thought of her sporting a wet T-shirt was about the only thing he could focus on at this point. He climbed up onto the dock and shook his head like a dog, splattering water on her.

"Stop it!" She backed up. "My God, does your hair ever look messed up?"

He shrugged, then flashed her his best smile. "The water's nice."

"I don't want to find out." She moved back even farther, holding her palms up to him.

"Oh, come on, Shauna."

"You try to push me in, I'll take you with me."

He chuckled. "Already wet."

"Travis, don't."

"Give me one good reason." He winked, jumping behind her, not allowing her off the dock, and backing her toward the lake.

"I don't have a change of clothes."

"I'll find you some." Only a few inches were left between them.

She bit her lip and looked over her shoulder. It was about the sexiest darn thing he'd ever seen. Visions of taking her in his arms and kissing her until they both begged for air almost overtook him. But then he was having too much fun acting like a teenager.

"I can't swim," she said.

"I don't believe you." He lunged forward. "Crap." The miscalculation about how quick she could be cost him, but the lake felt a little warmer this time. He opened his eyes in the moonlit water, making it easy for him to see the surface. She bent over, hands on knees, and he assumed she was looking for him. Thank God he could hold his breath for a long time. His feet squished in the seaweed, then he pushed off the bottom of the lake and surged up out of the water, grabbing her arms and yanking her in.

She cursed something as she hit the water.

He laughed, swimming for the dock and hoisting himself to a sitting position.

When she came up, she spit a mouthful of water at his chest. "Was that fun?" A spray of liquid hit him in the face from her splashing hand.

"Loads."

"Give me a hand."

He took her outstretched hand. "Oh, not fair," he muttered just before he gladly went under. Something about being in the cool lake on a starry night with a beautiful woman made him forget all about his job.

When he came up, she was waiting for him with a mouthful of water. "Truce?" she asked.

"Who gets the towel?"

"I can't believe you asked that." She chuckled as she hoisted herself up on the dock and grabbed the towel, rubbing it against her hair.

The quickening of his pulse at the sight of the moon shining against her light-brown hair caused his breath to hitch. As his eyes moved across her face, down her throat and to her chest, his pulse came to an abrupt halt. Her nipples were pressed hard against her T-shirt. She covered her breasts with the towel and frowned.

He snatched it away. "My mother taught me to share." All he wanted to do was gawk. No. He wanted to touch.

Violently, he dried his hair, all the while staring at her breasts. The increasing bulge in his wet jeans was decisively uncomfortable. So uncomfortable, it destroyed his good senses.

Catching her gaze, he inched closer, then dropped the towel to the dock.

Her eyes were apprehensive, but approachable. He had to taste her. Fully taste her. He knew she would taste like a woman should. Warm, soft, and…

He pressed his mouth against hers.

Her eyes fluttered closed, giving him permission to deepen the kiss.

He could feel his control begin to snap as he traced a path across her lips with his tongue. A mixture of fresh spring water and apples filled his taste buds as he probed the inside of her mouth.

Her mouth parted as her tongue greeted his, matching his gentle strokes.

The swell of her breast filled his hand. His thumb rubbed the hard nub through the wet fabric. She arched her back, pressing her breast more firmly into his palm. Her body responded to him, setting him on fire.

Unable to get close enough, he cupped her behind, pulling her firmly against him. He moved his kisses to her neck, licking off the lake droplets from her soft, supple skin. "So beautiful," he murmured.

"Travis!" His mother's voice filled the air, killing the moment.

"What?" His breathing was still labored, and his gaze heavy with desire as Shauna took a step back.

"Jake's on the phone for you," his mother called.

"Tell him I'll call him back. And we need a couple more towels." He took Shauna by the hand. "I'm sorry."

"Me, too." She sighed.

He couldn't tell if she was sorry about the kiss or getting interrupted again. Man, did Jake's timing suck.

Later, when it came time to head back to Albany, Travis felt an emptiness hit the pit of his stomach. Shauna had pulled away from him, keeping any conversation they had to small talk.

He had wanted to take her to his place, not her room. Working with her every day would certainly be a test of his manhood. She affected him on every level. She was the most dangerous kind of woman: a woman who could be his equal.

*B*y the time Sunday rolled around, Travis needed to get rid of some pent-up energy, as he called it. 'Sexual frustration' would be putting it mildly.

He held the phone in his hands. "Are you nuts?" he yelled at himself, slamming the phone down, knocking over a picture. The only person he could think of to call had been her.

She was the last person he should be calling in his present state of mind. And body. He dialed Jeff's number, another single agent who might be free for a game of tennis.

About an hour later, he paced at the fitness club, waiting for Jeff who was notorious for being late. Travis glanced at his watch. Okay, so he had a tendency to be early.

"Hey, thanks for the phone call. You saved my ass." Jeff smacked Travis on the back as he strolled into the club. "Women. Nothing you do is ever the right thing."

Travis cracked his neck. "I suppose."

"Not sure what I was drinking last night, but I brought home a dog, a stray dog who won't leave. That is, until you called."

Travis stretched, trying to ignore Jeff.

"How's the skirt?"

Travis wished he had decided on weightlifting by himself. "Agent Morgan's very intelligent. She'll make a fine agent." He bounced the ball, taking a nice, easy swing.

"Intelligent? Man, what about that body? How'd you luck out?" Jeff increased the speed of the ball like it was nothing.

Travis swung gently, keeping the pace of the warm-up slow, and ignoring Jeff's statement. You didn't need a good set of eyes to notice Shauna was a knockout.

"You think you'll make two years without making a pass at her?" Jeff practiced his serve.

One that was always tough to return.

"She's my partner. Just another agent doing *her* job." He swung harder, determined to get Jeff to shut up. He understood how important it was for a woman to be seen as an agent first, and a woman last.

"Yeah, I'll bet she can do a *job*."

Travis wound up and aimed for Jeff's crotch. The yellow ball barely missed its mark.

"Hey, watch it," Jeff barked.

"Say something like that again, and I'll do worse." Travis bounced the ball and hit it back to Jeff, nice and easy.

"Touchy," Jeff muttered. "Let's get the show on the road."

Travis played a decent game, but he still lost. And his mood soured even more. Jeff wasn't any different than other jerk males who just wanted to look at a pretty woman and take advantage of her. But hadn't he done that with Shauna? He kept trying to tell himself that he was different. Well, he was. He did respect her, certainly valued her as a fellow agent. But he couldn't ignore her as a woman either.

"Thanks again, that was fun." Jeff stretched out his arm. "Wanna go get a beer?"

"No, thanks. I've got some research to do."

"You still working on those rape cases?"

"A few." Travis hadn't kept his extracurricular activities to himself, but he didn't advertise them either. It tended to get him in trouble. But once Jeff had caught him copying shit he shouldn't have. Jeff had seemed genuinely interested in his research and even helped him out a few times.

"Do you ever think that maybe the girls go willingly in some of these cases?"

"Nothing willing about rape," Travis said.

"Oh, come on. Some of these girls prance around half-naked, almost begging for it."

"You're an asshole." Travis slammed the locker.

"I'm just saying that in today's world, any girl who hangs out in bus terminals, train stations, or the freaking drug store for that matter with her belly showing and her boobs bouncing has to know that men are going to notice, especially the bad guys."

Travis clenched his fist. "What the hell is that supposed to mean?"

"Simple: don't let your daughters dress like streetwalkers and parade around with the attitude like they're good and ready."

"You don't have a clue." Travis shoved Jeff to the side.

"Hey, look. I'm not condoning rape, okay? All I'm saying is that girls hear this shit all day long, and they still go off with these guys. I can't help but wonder how many of them are crying rape."

Travis blinked, forcing his fists apart. "I'm going pretend you didn't just say that." Travis slammed the locker room door, and in a few quick strides, he was outside heading for his truck. Travis knew his sister hadn't paraded around asking to be raped and killed.

6

Shauna lifted the mascara wand to her lashes with a shaking hand. The loneliness she'd endured on Sunday hadn't diminished by Monday morning. "Damn it." She grabbed a tissue and rubbed the blackness from her face, then pumped her fist and forced her hand to relax.

Sunday had been spent doing what she'd always done. Her routine had consisted of a good workout, a hot cup of coffee while reading the paper, and then a long search on the Internet. But while on the computer looking for any kind of clue that could lead her to her attacker, she realized just how pathetic her life had become.

She tossed her eyeliner into her cosmetic bag. Grabbing her purse, she headed out to her car in a huff.

Her heart raced, just as it did at five thirty when

she knew Travis would be at her door for their morning jog. He and his family had dulled her feelings of isolation for a short period of time. Until this past weekend, she hadn't known how lonely she'd been.

The sun shone strong in the dark-blue morning sky as the birds chirped in the cool spring air. She dug deep in her purse, eyes on nothing but her fingers searching for her keys.

Someone grabbed her arm.

Instinctively, she reached for her weapon and prepared to defend herself.

"Relax." She heard Travis's smooth voice. It sent warm shivers down her spine.

"You scared me."

"Sorry." He guided her across the street to where his truck was parked. "Get in. We got another one."

The blood in her body froze. "What do you mean?"

"Hotel downtown. Fifteen-year-old. Missing two days." He opened the door for her and touched her arm. "There's a note."

"That's new." She coughed, unable to concentrate on anything other than the pounding of her heart against her chest.

Moments later, she followed Travis into the despicable old hotel. Streetwalkers paced the hallways, yelling at the police that they were being harassed. The air was thick and stuffy with the pungent stench of five-day-old whiskey breath and rotten eggs.

"Here." He handed her a pair of latex gloves. Snapping them in place, she prayed her breakfast would stay in her stomach.

Travis turned and looked over his shoulder. "You ready?"

She nodded and held her stomach. This could still be her fate, if she didn't watch her back. A strong sensation of someone being behind her made her body stiffen and jerk, but she resisted the urge to glance over her shoulder.

She could still hear the killer's words echoing in her ears. He told her that after death he would take care of her. Make sure that God was willing to accept her because she hadn't sinned.

Hugging herself as her stomach hit her throat, she swallowed. She could taste the bile burning her esophagus.

"Glad you could make it," a familiar voice said.

"Can't say I'm thrilled. Hutchensen, you remember my new partner?"

"Sure do."

"Good to see you again." She stood still and scanned the room as her eyes watered from the rancid stench. Her head spun, and spots flickered about in front of her eyes. She tried to remove herself as best she could as her gaze followed Travis. He looked everywhere but at the body, and he talked to no one. Then he moved to the foot of the bed.

A faint gasp escaped her mouth. The body lay face up, eyes closed, and the smell of antiseptic filtering through Shauna's nose couldn't douse the aroma of death.

Nothing could kill that scent. It was a smell that lingered with you, stuck to you like a bad cigar. Her skin prickled as she felt death cling to her body, almost like it was trying to take her.

A dress lay neatly next to the victim, and a crown had been placed by her head. Small drops of blood dotted her stomach where a note had been tacked to her skin with a large safety pin.

"We'd like to believe it's the same guy, but the note's new," Hutchensen announced.

"Holy shit," Travis muttered. "Shauna, get over here." He motioned to her without looking up.

Swallowing hard, legs numb, she stumbled and stood behind Travis, bracing herself with a hand on his strong shoulder. She leaned over him and read the note out loud. "I'm right in front of you, behind you, next to you. I know who you are. Catch me if you can."

"What the hell does that mean?" someone said from behind her.

"It means we have a comedian on our hands," another officer barked. "Let's get this bagged and tagged and get on with the business of finding this psycho."

Hours later, the horror of the day lingered. She and Travis had spent the remainder of daylight going over information with the Albany, State, and Troy Police Departments. They had more paperwork than they knew what to do with, but there was good news. They now had three cases that were believed to be the same guy. Enough to give this guy a name. He would be known as the Princess Killer.

Shauna didn't like the name much, but she knew it was the same guy who'd raped her. And now she had the opportunity to nail him. Hopefully she looked different enough that he wouldn't be able to tell who she was. Eventually, she would have to tell Travis, but not yet. She needed more time to remember.

Digging into her purse for her key, she became keenly aware that something wasn't right. She glanced over her shoulder and then down the hall. With her eyes locked on her open door, she took out her weapon and held it to her side as she crept down the hallway.

She grabbed her phone and hit speed dial.

"Brown, here."

"Someone broke into my room," she whispered. "I'm in the hallway; the door's open."

"Go back down to the lobby and wait for me. I'm on my way." The phone went dead.

Quietly, she moved down the hallway, again with

her back to the wall. While she felt confident in her abilities as an agent, going it alone would be a classic rookie mistake. One she wasn't willing to make when her life was on the line. She tucked her gun in her purse and waited by the door for Travis.

Jumping from his truck, he jogged into the lobby and took her by the arm. "You see anything else?"

She shook her head. "Just that my door was open. No maids or construction workers in sight." She pulled out her weapon and followed him down the hall.

He turned and motioned to her, then pushed the door open.

She backed him up as he moved about the room, opening closets and heading into the bedroom and bathroom.

"Is anything missing?" he asked as he holstered his gun.

"Looks like whoever it was had been looking for something...specific." She took a good look around at her clothes that lay strewed about the floor. "My journal?" Pieces of ripped paper were scattered at her feet. She opened the nightstand.

Oh my God.

The journal felt heavy in her trembling hands. Fear paralyzed her ability to think. She sat back on the bed. The mattress squeaked and jerked as he sat down next to her and put a comforting arm around her. She took deep breaths as she flipped through the pages. How could the killer know?

"What's missing?"

"Random pages." She jumped from the bed. "Oh, crap."

"What?"

"I have more journals." She dropped to her knees in front of the closet and pulled out the box she kept them in. She sucked in nothing, she couldn't breathe.

The box was empty.

"He knows," she whispered. "He knows," she repeated, trying to hide the sense of defeat she felt deep in her heart.

---

*T*ravis knelt down beside her. This was beyond his comprehension. He didn't know how to deal with it, and he sure as hell couldn't explain it. Somehow the killer just upped the ante, making this even more personal.

"What does he know?"

Soft sobs fell from her lips. "He's close," she whispered.

"Shauna." He took her by the shoulders and shook her. "What does he know?"

Abruptly, she stood and started to pace.

"Come on. What's going on inside that head of yours?"

She stopped and glared at him. "He has my personal thoughts about who I think he might be. My profile of him. How I've gone about looking for him most of my life."

"Whoa, there. Hold up. Rewind that." He cracked his neck. "Most of your life? As in years?"

"Years." She stared him down, as if she was daring him to say something. "Those journals. He might be able to use them against us."

"What's in them that I don't know? What are you keeping from me?" He took out her suitcase and placed it on the bed, dumping the clothes on the floor in it.

"I've jotted down what we've been up to." She placed her hands on her hips. "What are you doing?"

"Packing...what does it look like?" He held the suitcase open and in one swift motion, he dumped the things lining the top of the dresser into the suitcase. Her birth control pills didn't go unnoticed.

"And just where am I going?" Much to his relief, the confidence in her voice had come back.

"To my apartment." He turned to her.

Stunned didn't begin to describe her gaping jaw. He nodded. "No way in hell do I want a lecture from my mother if she ever found out I let you stay here after this."

"Leave your mother out of this. I think I can handle myself." She sneered at him.

"No shit, but the Princess Killer knows we're onto

him. He's going to come after us." He took her by the wrist and stood so close to her that it caused his heart to skip a beat. "I think we both know this killer just claimed his territory, and we're both safer if we're together." His nose almost touched hers, and her eyes dug into his soul.

"I can't stay with you." Her chest rose up and down in perfect unison with his.

"No one has to know. We'll leave your car here. It will look as though you still live here. But if you think I'll let you stay alone after this, you've got another thing coming."

"Don't you dare dictate to me."

"Oh, for the love of God, be reasonable. Some psycho just broke into your room. Do you want to end up like the others?"

Her eyes widened, and she swallowed. "Of course...not." Her face paled.

"Jesus, Shauna. I'm sorry." He pulled her close to him, forcing her hands to his shoulders. "But you understand being alone is stupid, and you are not stupid."

He traced her profile with his knuckles and stared into her stubborn, but welcoming blue eyes. A feeling stirred in him that he thought had died long ago. His partner brought it to life, a thought that snapped him back to reality.

He stepped back, still holding her hips. "I'm sorry."

"I can't stay with you."

"Then I'll stay with you. I mean it. From this point on, we're glued together." He took a deep breath.

"If I were a man?" she questioned. "Travis, it shouldn't matter. I'm a field agent, just like you. Please don't hold my brief moment of panic against me."

"Oh, please. You're a first and skirt, and my responsibility. Now finish packing or I'll throw you over my shoulder and carry you out if I have to."

Shauna opened her mouth, but nothing came out.

"Shit." Travis tossed one of her shirts at her suitcase and walked out of the bedroom. "Nice move." He paced while waiting for her. The only thing Shauna was to him was his partner. Damn hot partner at that.

Now his freaking roommate. "Let's get a move on," he yelled toward the bedroom, wondering how the hell he would get through the next few days without losing his job or getting slapped.

Shauna started stuffing her belongings in her suitcase. *Damn him.* How could she let Travis affect her? The fact that the killer had to know she was Jane Doe was the only reason she would stay with him. Alone, she was a sitting duck. When she'd leapt from the killer's moving car all those years ago, he told her he'd find her and finish what he'd started.

Her hands trembled as she fumbled with the zipper on her suitcase. Then the tears came. She hated crying.

"Hey. It's okay." Strong arms wrapped around her.

With an angry shove, she pushed him away.

"What's going on?" Travis took the suitcase from her.

"I'm pissed this guy terrifies me, considering the badge I carry."

"I'd be more worried if this guy didn't scare the shit out of you." He handed her purse to her and guided her out of the room and down the hallway.

"You don't understand."

"Yeah. I do." He glanced at her with accepting eyes. "We're on the case, and he's enjoying fucking with us."

"I don't like being fucked with."

"Me neither," he said. "We'll have to make appearances here, and as far as the bureau is concerned, you still live here. Got it?" He gave her a commanding look.

Not another word was said until they reached his apartment. Grateful, Shauna used the quiet to try to figure out how the killer knew about her. And how she was going to tell Travis who she really was.

"I can hear your wheels spinning." He opened the

door to his apartment for her, carrying her bag. "Plan on filling me in?"

She glanced around the family room. The last time she'd been in his apartment, she'd been too immersed in him to notice how nicely the room had been decorated. The new furniture was accented with deep colors, and he even had some plants near the front window. Travis Brown had a soft, sensitive side. And that made him even sexier.

"Shauna?"

"Thought left me." Did it ever. And it was replaced with thoughts of Travis holding her, kissing her, and comforting her. Not thoughts she should be equating with her partner. The only thoughts that should be going through her mind were those related to nabbing a rapist.

But she'd rather notice Travis. And she did just that as she followed him into the spare bedroom. It, too, had been impeccably decorated. He used dark, masculine earth tones that made her want to take his aftershave lotion and spray the bed covers with it. She blushed.

"We have to share a bathroom. I need at least forty-five minutes in there." Effortlessly, he tossed her suitcase on the bed. A pillow bounced off.

"I can dry my hair and put on my makeup in here. I'll take it first and then be out of your way in less than fifteen." What the hell was she doing? Protecting herself from a ruthless rapist and killer.

She shivered, then rubbed her arms with her hands. "Whoever this guy is, he knows we're working together, and he's watching us."

His long finger traced her jawline. "He knows a lot more than we've given him credit for. I'm afraid the killings will increase, and he's going to try to rub our noses in it." His eyes scanned over her face. "You're trembling."

"He has my thoughts. That journal had things I've put together trying to connect him to Marie, to others." *He knows who I am,* she wanted to scream.

Travis rubbed his jaw. "Why have you been doing that?"

"When I did the case study in college, I accused the professor of being incompetent."

Travis snickered.

"Don't laugh. That happened to get me in a whole heap of trouble. I've gotten emotionally involved." Emotionally involved, but not in the way she was portraying herself.

"You're not supposed to let that happen."

"Yeah, well, take a good look in the mirror."

He smiled. "I'll order a pizza."

"I'd like to take a bath first, if you don't mind."

"Not at all." He squeezed her shoulder and then waltzed out of her new quarters.

Moments later, Shauna twisted the hot water faucet to the tub, letting the bathroom fill with a dense cloud of steam. She liked her bath hot, almost scalding. Her toes rippled the water as she settled into the bubbles. Letting her head rest on the tub, she tried to rid her mind of all the bad memories that haunted her daily existence. She wanted to cleanse her mind, body, and soul. If nothing else, she would try to feel safe. Something she hadn't felt since...well, ever.

Taking a deep breath, she let her eyelids flutter closed. Her body demanded a rest. A faint knock at the door made her realize the water had become lukewarm.

"Shauna? You fall in?" she heard him call.

"I'm coming," she said, stepping out of the tub. Quickly, she dried herself and threw on her sweats. Taking a good look at herself in the mirror, she adjusted her ponytail high on her head. "Why do I care?" she said softly. He had seen her without makeup before.

"Pizza here?" she asked, entering the kitchen, trying to act nonchalant, as if this were all normal. It must not have been working because he chuckled, pouring some soda.

"You don't drink much, do you?" she asked.

"Got me in trouble when I lived in New York City. Almost lost my job. Did lose my focus. I decided it wasn't worth it, but I do like a beer now and then. What about you?" He handed her a slice of pizza on a napkin.

"My dad was the town drunk, and I don't like

losing control." She bit into the pizza. "Oh, God. This is good."

She got the feeling he was staring at her as she stuffed her face. Her hunger had gone unnoticed until she smelled pizza that could only have come from Capri's. She wiped her mouth with a napkin and turned to face him. "What?"

"You're beautiful." He continued staring.

Was this guy nuts? She glanced down at her oversized FBI training sweatpants. "Thanks, I think."

He took the pizza from her hand, tossed it on the counter, and then moved so close to her that she could hear his heart beating. "We have a huge problem," he said, tracing a path across her bottom lip.

'Huge' could only mean one thing. She glanced down.

"Not exactly what I was referring to," he said with an amused chuckle.

"Ugh." What was her problem?

When he cupped her face and searched her eyes, amusement had been replaced with passion. "I want you," he said with soft words.

"No."

He dropped his hands to his sides. "You feel the same way."

"Yes, and then very much a big, fat no." She slid from his intense stare. "I'm going to bed." Abruptly, she turned and marched herself into her new room. No way would she finish this conversation. It was absurd. Even if she did find him attractive, she had to work with him.

———————

*T*ravis entered the bathroom after he cleaned up from the pizza. Another anal habit his mother had taught him. "Christ." The whole room smelled like bottled sunshine that came from the lake on a hot summer day. It smelled like her, and he could most definitely drown in her wake.

Quickly, he got himself ready for bed, trying to rid himself of the mounting pressure in his boxers. He was harder than he had ever been in his life with no relief in sight. "Damn it." He dropped the toothpaste on the floor. *Huge* would be an understatement at this point. Painful would be a better descriptor. Hopefully, once in his own room, and away from everything she left behind, the pressure would lessen.

But that didn't happen. He tossed and turned and uttered a few curses. Then Travis just gave up and stared at the ceiling. The only thing that could get Shauna off his mind was a psychotic rapist and murderer.

A murderer who had made it very clear he knew Travis was onto something, and he was going to use Shauna to get to him. But why Shauna?

The journal pages. Travis had to find out what

Shauna had written in those journals. He grabbed his cell and punched Jake Hanson's number.

"Jake Hanson's phone," a female voice answered.

"Lana?"

"Hi, Travis. Jake said he caught you kissing some gorgeous woman out on the lake. Says she's your partner."

"Oh, she's my partner all right. Hope I didn't wake anyone up."

"Jake's trying to help settle Brent and Kyle down. So, do tell."

"Nothing to tell."

"Come on. You were kissing her."

Travis shifted under his sheets. "She's good-looking, but nothing's going on. You're becoming as bad as my mother."

"Yeah, well. You're a likeable kind of guy. I take it you want to talk with Jake?"

"Actually, I like talking with you."

"God, you're such a flirt. Hey, honey, it's Gumby Boy."

Travis shook his head. That woman would never let him forget his stupid youth.

"What's up?" Jake had spent fifteen years as a Green Beret working in top-secret government stuff that he was never allowed to talk about. Travis knew Jake had spent a few years chasing down members of Al-Qaeda in some remote area, but something happened, and Jake retired. Now he ran his own private investigating firm, and constantly bugged Travis to join him.

"You know anyone with the Saratoga Police?"

"As a matter of fact, I do. Why?"

"Would you mind asking him to do a little digging?"

"I never mind. Who?"

"Shauna Morgan."

"You're going to dig on your own partner?"

"No, you are. She's been collecting information for years on my guy. She even did a paper on my sister's file in school."

"Hmm. That's interesting."

"That's all you have to say?" Travis stared at Jane Doe's picture on his ceiling.

"What do you want me to say? She's your partner."

"Don't you find it odd she's spent so much time on this?" Travis asked.

"I suppose. Have you thought about asking her?"

"Of course not, that would be too obvious. Besides, if she's hiding something from me, she'd still lie."

"Have a little more faith in your partner," Jake remarked.

"I have faith in my instincts…and you."

"Gee, thanks. I'll let you know what I find out." The phone went dead. Jake had a way of hanging up when he was done, regardless of the other person.

"Thanks." Travis turned out the light and prayed for sleep. Slowly, it came to him. That was until an ear-piercing scream came from his guest room.

Springing from his bed, he grabbed his gun and took off toward another scream.

"No! Leave me alone!" Shauna sat in the bed and punched at the air. "Stop! You're hurting me! No! Please. No," she whimpered.

"Shauna?" Travis put his gun on the nightstand, sitting on the edge of the bed.

"Please don't hurt me." She sobbed.

"It's okay." He pulled her close. "I'm here. No one's going to hurt you."

She continued to cry, wrapping her arms around him. She held him tight and shook like a scared baby animal left alone to fend for itself.

He tucked himself in bed with her and stroked her hair until he knew she had fallen into a deep sleep. "What happened to you?" he whispered at her temple, planting a kiss there.

Her secret might be as simple as someone hurt her.

But who?

And why?

7

God, *that smell.* Shauna inhaled deeply, taking in a scent she could wake to every day. It smelled like a mixture of early morning mist rising from the lake and soft pine from the mountaintop on a cool, fall morning. It smelled like Travis.

She opened her eyes in shock. That delicious aroma was right under her nose.

A faint gasp escaped her lips before she could cover her mouth. The male version of Sleeping Beauty lay curled up next to her, his hair perfectly rumpled. Why the hell was he in her bed? She didn't remember him joining her. Worse, she didn't seem to mind.

She blinked and then looked beneath the sheets. Thank God, she was fully clothed. With a sigh of relief, she crept from under the covers, grabbed her running clothes, and then snuck out of the bedroom.

The clock on the wall said it was six. She'd have plenty of time for a run, but a better idea came to mind. She peeked back into the bedroom. He lay on his side, one hand tucked under the pillow, the other where her body had been. He looked peaceful. God, he was a perfect specimen.

Don't do it, Morgan. She tiptoed toward Travis's bedroom. You could learn so much from what a man kept in his room, and she just couldn't help herself. Taking in a deep breath, she pushed open the door and scanned. Way too neat for her taste. Not a stitch of clothing lined the floor. He had a few magazines on his nightstand, but even those were organized.

She glanced around the room and had to admire his taste as she ran her hand across his hunter green bedspread. The walls were a lighter green, and the curtains were blue and green with some khaki folded in. She chuckled. Travis Brown was unique.

She picked up the latest fishing magazine. "Oh, my." She tossed that one aside and glanced at some French cooking magazine. "Fishing to cooking to... well." She laughed, tossing the fishing magazine over his girlie mag, mildly amused.

A warm sensation filled her body. Just thinking about him sent her hormones into overdrive. In hopes of stifling her inappropriate reaction to her partner, she glanced at the ceiling. "Oh, God." Pictures of girls stared down at her. "Good, God. Is that...oh shit, it is."

Without a second thought, she climbed on his bed and glossed over her own picture, which was next to Marie's and slightly separate from all the other girls she knew to be *his* victims. So many more than she'd found, but Travis had been doing this longer. Thank God he knew the real killer still lurked behind a dark shadow.

"What are you doing?" Travis asked.

The bed didn't hold her footing and she fell over, landing on her butt. She bounced.

"What are you doing?" he asked again.

He had the sheet from her bed wrapped around his waist and a gun in his hand. And his hair was... messed up, but still looked damned good. Not fair. She ran a hand through her hair, then squinted. "Care to explain?"

"Victims who I think were murdered and raped by the same guy, but no one else does." His tone was terse.

She shook her head. "Not that. Why were you in my bed?" She waved her arms, feeling her face flush. She tried to keep an angry look, but she really wanted to run her fingers through his thick, dark hair.

In less than two paces, he stood in front of her, placed his gun on the nightstand, and continued to look at her. His intent was unmistakably sexual. "You had a bad dream."

"So? Everyone has them."

"You screamed; I came running. I didn't leave."
He shrugged.

"So much for being a gentleman." She had to bite
her tongue, when what she really wanted to do was
laugh. So much about this man intrigued her, and not
just professionally.

"I was a gentleman." He inched closer. "I didn't
do anything but this." His soft lips barely brushed
against her temple. "But I wanted to do this."
Cupping her face, he pressed his mouth hotly against
hers.

She inhaled sharply, then gripped his shoulders,
feeling dizzy. She closed her eyes and glided her hands
down his strong, bare chest. Clasping her fingers
around his back, she welcomed his tongue in her
mouth.

Abruptly, he pried his lips from hers, hands still
cupping her face. "We can't do this." His voice
sounded dark and low. "My job. Our jobs." His hands
dropped to his sides.

"You should have thought of that five minutes
ago." Shauna touched her lips. She'd never felt like
this before. How could his kiss tell her that he would
understand?

She sidestepped him and headed out of his
room.

"Shauna? Your dream…who hurt you?"

"What?" She stopped at his door but didn't turn
around.

"In your dream, you begged someone not to hurt you."

She felt his breath on her neck before his hands gently touched her shoulders, turning her to face him.

Her eyes burned. What did he know? Or think he knew? She'd had bad dreams before, but they didn't plague her. And she didn't remember having one last night.

When she looked into his eyes, she knew she would never be able to directly lie to him. "I was raped as a teenager."

"By who?"

"A stranger. And no, he was never caught."

"Are you looking for him?" he asked, his eyes narrowed in suspicion.

Her stomach leaped into her throat. She swallowed and turned from him. "I never really saw his face, but he's part of the reason I became an agent." She paused, then turned. "He's why I studied your sister's case and some others. I wanted to understand him, but there is no understanding." She forced back the tears that threatened to drip down her cheeks.

"What did he do to you?" His voice rang out full of anger and contempt.

"He raped me," she answered truthfully.

"Trust me, murder would come easily to me if anyone tried to hurt you again." He lowered his chin.

She believed him and that scared her. Even more

so, that his words comforted her. No way should the idea of murder comfort her in any way. Yet there it was, and she felt safe. So safe, she wrapped her arms around his solid middle and rested her head on his shoulder, nuzzling her lips against his neck. "I can't change what happened, but I can move past it and live my life."

"Are you sure this is living?"

"I'm helping other people like me. I call that living."

"All right," he said. "If you ever want to talk about it—"

"I'm fine, really. I've had therapy, and in many ways, this job is therapeutic."

"Running my ass off is therapeutic. Want to join me?"

"Definitely." On impulse, she flicked her fingers through his hair.

He grabbed her wrist, kissing her hand. "Watch it, sweetheart." He winked. "You're going to get me fired. Get out so I can change." He shoved her out the door.

Fumbling with her laces, she couldn't get the image of Travis wrapped in only a sheet out of her head. He had to be naked under that white cloth. That meant he had to have been just as naked when he'd slept next to her.

She should have been mad as hell, but she wasn't. And she didn't understand why. She stretched her back, making a mental note that her first phone call of the day would be to the rental office. She had to know if she got that apartment down the street. She hoped Travis would feel that was close enough, because right now, they were way too close.

By Friday, Travis couldn't take much more. He had Shauna and her damn scent following him wherever he went. The fresh smell of violets filled his office, his bathroom, and even his damn truck. Thank God they had been scheduled for court that afternoon. The sport coat helped hide the mounting pressure below his waist.

"You ready?" He stood behind his desk and barked at her. He didn't mean to sound so demanding, but she'd climbed deep into his skin. And he had to work with her. Not going to be easy without ripping off her clothes.

"What crawled up your ass?" She gave him a pointed look.

"You don't want me to elaborate here." He turned toward the door.

Steve leaned against the doorjamb, looking at his fingernails. "Trouble in paradise?" He gave Travis a smug grin.

"What's up?" Travis moved to stand in front of him. Steve was a moron and a jerk. Not to mention crude and insulting and should never be trusted with a lady. *Get a grip.* Travis mentally shook himself.

"Heard over the radio they found a teenage girl in Washington Park." Travis caught a hint of sorrow in Steve's eyes. "Looks like your man." He squeezed Travis's shoulder.

Travis glanced at the hand on his shoulder, blinked, and then looked at Shauna. She stood, but fear lurked behind her eyes.

"Brown. Morgan," Scott called as he maneuvered his way around Steve. "I need you two in Washington Park. Steve, you cover for Travis in court."

"Sure." Steve glanced at Shauna. "It's ugly out there. No place for a woman."

"I am an FBI Agent," she said confidently.

Travis had to stand back when he really wanted to deck the ignorant ass. "What happened?"

"They actually think it's the Princess Killer, even though there's no dress or crown."

"Then how are the police linking it to our guy?" Shauna asked.

"A note."

"I take it we're on the case?" she asked.

"You're there as part of the Joint Task Force. You let the police do their job. Give them what we have, officially. Later, I'll look at what you've dug up. I take it you didn't listen to me and brought her in on this anyway?"

Travis looked from Shauna to Scott and smiled. "I

figured. Go. Then go home. It's late. Bring what you have in on Monday morning."

---

*T*ravis reflected on the crime scene during the drive home. It didn't have much, except the note. The note disturbed him. The first part had been identical to the last one, except there was an additional line that said, 'Not everyone is who they say they are. Some of us are living a lie.'

But who was the killer talking about? The killer himself? Or someone else?

He glanced at Shauna. Something didn't add up. Whatever it was she was hiding, he figured it had to do with this case. He needed to get it from her without alienating her. He turned to see her looking out the window, deep in thought.

"I can hear you thinking over there. What's up?" The truck jerked as he pulled up in front of his favorite little store.

"You're not going to like this."

"I don't like rapists and murders much anyway."

"The paper the note was on is the same paper that's in my journals." She shifted in the seat.

"Huh?" He blinked and then started again. "How can you be sure?"

"I'm not sure it's from one of my journals, but it's the same brand. The lines, the colors, and the numbers all match. Even the perforation is doubled like mine."

Travis slammed the truck back in gear, glanced over his shoulder, and punched the gas pedal.

"What are you doing?" She touched his forearm.

"We're going to go back to my place, collect all our stuff, and head to the lake for the weekend. I need to talk with my buddy Jake. A fresh set of eyes might help."

"I can't go away with you for the weekend. What if we get called in or something?"

"Then it will be good that we're together."

The drive to the lake had been quiet, but that was okay with Travis. He'd been having crazy thoughts that Shauna might actually know where Jane Doe was hiding.

"Don't your parents live down that road?" Shauna pointed as they passed Rockefeller Road.

"We're going to Jake's place first. I'd like to give him what we've got, that way by Sunday, maybe he'll have an angle on what we might have missed." God, Travis hoped so. He had a sick feeling that the killings would just keep coming now. For some reason, the killer chose this time to get nervy. Hopefully that meant he would get caught, and soon. Travis really didn't want to see another dead body.

"Nice place," Shauna commented.

He nodded, taking her arm as they headed down a pathway to Jake's home. "Hey there, Katie."

"Gumby!" Katie jumped from Lana's arms and ran out the door toward them.

"Gumby?" Shauna lifted a brow.

"Don't ask." Travis picked Katie up and twirled her around. "Does she even know my name?" He glanced from Katie to Lana. "Lana, this is my partner, Shauna Morgan. Shauna, this is Lana, Jake's wife, and my cousin." Travis kissed Lana's cheek.

"Nice to meet you. Come on in. Jake's in the family room with the twins."

"I show 'em, Mommy." Katie tugged at Travis. "She's pretty." Katie winked. "Daddy say you need girfrend."

"That's enough, pumpkin." Jake scooped up Katie. "Welcome to the nut house. This is Brent and Kyle." Jake pointed to a playpen that housed two babies.

"Oh, my. They're adorable." Shauna leaned over the playpen.

Travis bent over and lifted one of the boys in his arms. "How old?"

"Three months now." Jake put Katie down.

Travis blew raspberries on the baby's belly, and the baby roared, laughing. The other one cried.

"Brent gets jealous. I gotcha, little buddy." Jake lifted the other boy in his arms.

"May I?" Shauna stretched out her hands.

"Sure." Jake handed her the baby, giving Travis an inquisitive glance.

She cooed with him, tickling the little boy, making him belly laugh. She looked at Travis and smiled, then gave her attention back to the baby.

His heart jumped and tightened with a rush of an overwhelming sense of connectedness to her. It raged through his body and mind, giving into ideas he thought he'd buried. Watching her with the little boy sent him down a path where he'd placed a roadblock. She made him want to knock it down.

He couldn't take that fork, and certainly not with her. Right now, they were too good together as partners. She was smart and added things to his investigation that were invaluable in tracking down Jane Doe, which would lead him to his sister's killer.

"Okay, who goes to bed first?" Lana asked, entering the room. "Looks like Brent made himself a friend."

"He's got good taste," Jake commented.

"Just like his father." Lana planted a wet kiss on her husband.

Travis cleared his throat.

"Get over yourself, Gumby Boy, and give me my baby back," Lana teased. He gave Kyle a kiss and handed him to his mother.

"Can I help?" Shauna asked as the baby in her arms smiled and squealed in delight.

"If you want. But I'll warn you, they can be stubborn mules, just like their father."

"Oh, I can handle stubborn." Shauna glanced at Travis.

"I bet you can." Lana laughed, motioning Shauna toward the stairs.

"Nothing going on, my ass." Jake nodded toward his office. "Thought I might have to lift your jaw up off the floor."

"Knock it off, okay?" Travis cracked his neck, then sat in the chair across from a big, old wooden desk. He dumped a file down in front of Jake.

"That bad?"

"I'd lose my job. I won't risk it."

"I think you already have." Jake opened the file.

"Have not. I haven't touched her."

Jake's eyes lifted from the paper he held in his hands. "I see."

"Can we just focus on that file and not my love life?"

Jake dipped his eyes back to the paper. Silence filled the room. He just kept flipping through the file. "Looks like your killer's getting antsy."

"Tell me something I don't know."

"You know him."

"So he keeps telling me." Travis stood and paced.

Jake pushed his chair back. "He knows you'll be called, so he's leaving you hints. I doubt he's at the scene when you are, but he knows you're coming. What I can't figure out is how Shauna fits into this."

"What are you thinking?" Travis made eye contact.

"I'm thinking he knows her, too. And I mean personally. I have nothing but my gut reaction, but it seems since you two started working together, he's started playing games with you— both of you. That bothers the shit out of me."

Jake hadn't told him anything he wasn't already thinking. But Jake's opinion meant a lot to Travis, and his validation took away the guilt that he had about checking out his partner. "Any info from Saratoga?"

"Just basic facts. Her parents are divorced. Father remarried. Town drunk. Brother disappeared. Believed to be involved in drugs. That's about it for now. He's still digging."

Travis could hear Lana and Shauna coming toward the office, so he stopped talking. Thus far, all he had was validation that he was moving on the right track. That was enough for him.

Now to figure out how in God's name he was going to spend the night in one of the most sensual places on earth, with the hottest woman on the planet, and not touch her.

A few hours later, Shauna sat on the front deck of Travis's family home and stared at the sky. There were so many stars that the lake rippled with the bright glow, making the moon dance softly across the tiny waves as they gently crashed against the shoreline. She closed her eyes and took in a deep breath. She could still smell the babies. God, she loved babies.

She opened her eyes in anger. Her rapist still had so much control over her life. Hate was too mild a word to describe her feelings for the monster who'd taken away not only her innocence, but her womanhood. Her entire self. Her therapist had warned her about coming home and how her inner demons would resurface. It was important she pull back all the control and take charge. Live her life. The only problem, by coming back here and working with Travis, her life ended up back in the past. Or maybe she'd never really left.

"I hope you're not thinking about me?" Travis pulled up a chair and sat down next to her, two beers in hand. "It's been a long day, want one?"

She took the beer and swigged it. Swallowing hard, she held back a cough. It had been a long time since she'd had a beer. She forgot how bad it tasted, but she needed to relax. "Thanks."

"I've got wine if you'd prefer."

She turned to him. The moonlight hit his eyes and knocked her senseless. "Next time tell me that before I start on this." She held the beer up and studied him as he turned and sipped his beer. "You like kids, don't you?" she asked, taking another sip of courage.

"What's not to like about them?" He cracked his knuckles.

"I hate that."

He did it again and smiled.

Damn him. She smiled back. He was way too cute. "Want any? Kids, I mean." She turned and felt her cheeks flush. Why would she get so personal with him? Personal was dangerous.

He took a sip of beer and seemed to ponder the question. "I did once." His sip became a chug.

"What happened to change your mind?"

"My fiancée decided that the timing was off and had an abortion." He tipped his beer and finished it.

"Without your knowledge?" She swung her feet to the side of the lounge chair, putting her elbows on her knees and resting her chin in her hands.

"Oh, she told me. But I couldn't change her mind. She had this plan." He tilted his chin. "We were supposed to get married when she finished law school, first kid two years after she made partner, then maybe a second two years after that, but she wasn't sold on having more than one." Travis tried not to laugh.

"You asked this woman to marry you?" Shauna's voice went up an octave.

Travis batted her nose. "Nope."

"Now I'm really confused."

"The plan. It was all a part of her plan. I thought I loved her, so the plan seemed to be okay with me. I just thought when she got pregnant, 'The Plan' would be adjusted. She didn't."

"Where's she now?" Shauna looked down at her lap. Travis's finger danced on her knee.

"Working as a lawyer in New York City. She married another lawyer, and I'm sure as soon as she makes partner, she might have a kid."

"She's a fool," Shauna said.

"No fool. Her plan's working just fine for her. I just wasn't the right guy. Too bad for me I found that out too late." Travis stood, placing his hands on the railing and looking out over the lake.

Shauna joined him, leaning slightly against his arm. "Because of her, you no longer want to have a family?"

"It's not entirely her fault. Gina and I knew each other in high school. She knew my sister, and I thought she understood my drive." He rubbed his jaw. "I need to find Jane Doe." He shot Shauna a cold stare that shocked her system. All the kindness he usually carried had been replaced with pure rage and anguish. She looked into the depths of a man who would stop at nothing to get what he wanted.

"She holds the key. We need to flush her out."

"Leave the 'we' out of it." Her stomach churned with the beer hitting the back of her throat. "I know what it's like to walk around and wonder if your attacker is following you, waiting for the right time to do it again. I won't put her in that position." *First lie,* she thought to herself.

"She's already out there, and we have the power to protect her." Travis's voice changed. She hated it when he used the voice of reason without knowing the effect he had on her.

"She may not even be alive." She wanted that to be true. Jane Doe had died for her the night she snuck away and went back to being Shauna Morgan. She touched his arm. "Even if she is alive, I understand her. I know what it's like to have the world push you to identify your rapist. I couldn't. I closed my eyes and what little I did see, I have tucked so far back in my mind that I'm not sure I'll ever be able to remember everything."

His hand rested against her cheek, and he looked deep into her eyes. "Don't you want to make sure that bastard pays for what he did to you?"

"For all I know, he has. He could be in jail right now." She blinked. Now that was a big lie.

"And that's good enough for you?"

"Of course not!" Rage coursed through her veins, igniting her vengeance. "I want the bastard to pay. I'd love to cut his balls off myself, but that's not the point."

Travis smiled. "What is the point?"

She opened her mouth just as the light bulb went on. She calmed herself a little and then spoke clearly, without anger. "This guy now has a name. He's going make national headlines. If Jane Doe figures this is her attacker, she will either get scared and hide or come to us. I bet she comes to us, eventually."

She studied him as he processed the information.

"I need another beer," he muttered, opening the slider. In a flash, he closed it.

Shauna knew him well enough to know he would chew on that for a few and realize she had a point. Travis was a lot of things, but he never shot down a reasonable explanation. She won that small battle, but she knew there would be more.

8

Travis popped the cork off the wine bottle and poured a glass. He'd stick to the beer, but it was obvious Shauna really didn't like it. If she didn't drink the wine, fine by him. He'd finish it for her. Getting drunk might be a good idea.

Why had he told her about Gina? And why did she make him stand at attention every damned time he looked at her? He needed to deaden himself from the waist down.

To make matters worse, she made way too many valid points. Ever since he and Gina had broken up, he'd sworn off smart women, and he had been doing a good job at that. Smart women were nothing but trouble. Before you knew it, they were running your life, telling you what to do and when to do it.

He lifted the glass, spilling some of the wine onto the counter. *Damn.* He put the glass down and filled it back up. Shaking his head, he tapped the sliding glass door.

Shauna opened the door, taking the wine glass from him. "Trying to get me drunk?" She seemed to be fighting off a smile.

"Nope, just me." He touched her glass with his bottle, then took a gulp. He could get drunk from looking at her. "Why do you have to be so beautiful?" He sipped his beer, almost choking on his own words.

"Thank you, I think." She took a small sip of the wine and then put it on the table. Looking down, she fiddled with her rings.

"You don't think you're beautiful, do you?" He lifted her chin.

"I don't think I'm ugly. I just wish it wasn't about gender all the time."

"I don't follow." He picked up her glass. "It's much prettier from the sun deck." He motioned toward the lake.

"There's no sun." She took her glass from him and put her other hand in the one he offered.

"Okay, moon deck. Either way, it's really nice right on the lake." Travis guided her down the path and up the stairs. He placed fluffy cushions on each of the chaise lounge chairs, sat, and then crossed his ankles. She followed suit, and they enjoyed the night sounds of the lake and the bright moonlit sky, saying nothing.

It didn't matter that no words passed between

them, because the mounting pressure in his pants had become almost unbearable, making it impossible to utter anything coherent. He turned to look at the cause. She was smiling at him.

"What?"

"Lana told me something funny."

"I can only imagine."

"She said you could do this with both legs." Shauna lifted her leg and dropped it behind her head.

Travis cleared his throat. He stared at her for a full minute, feeling the blood rush to unspeakable places.

"I'll do it if you do it." She smiled at him, lifting her other leg about five inches off the chair.

He blinked. "No way, you can't." Oh, but he wanted to see her do it.

"I can."

"On the count of three." Travis adjusted himself in the chair. He couldn't believe he was going to do this. It had been years since he had performed this stunt in front of a bunch of giddy girls, giving him the nickname Gumby Boy.

He knew he could still do it. He stretched every day to keep limber. Being flexible had its advantages in the field, but he never showed anyone, not anymore. But right now, he'd do just about anything to see her with both her feet behind her head. "One, two, three." He lifted both legs, reached for his ankles, and shoved them behind his head.

He watched in amazement, while she gracefully

raised her other leg behind her head, without the use of her hands.

"I think I just met my match." Carefully so as not to upset the tender balance in his pants, he used his hands to lower his legs. "Can you do a center split?"

She nodded, lowering her legs and jumping off the chair. "Count of three?"

"Can't I just watch you?" He sipped his beer, trying to hide his excitement. He wanted to watch her do a lot of things.

"Nuh-uh." She pulled him from the chair.

"I haven't stretched," he protested. "I don't think I'm as flexible as you."

"You're just chicken." She giggled as she started to slide.

"Is that a dare?" He stared at her, gently stretching his legs.

"I don't think you can do it," she teased.

That did it. Travis Brown was never one to pass on a dare. "Oh, honey, watch this." He joined her but couldn't quite get all the way down. He stayed like that for a moment, stretching, and decided it was more fun to watch. He sat back, crossed his legs, and admired her. She could do a center split and then some. Her legs were as wide as her smile, her elbows on the deck, her chin resting nicely in her palms.

"Nose?" he asked, pointing to his own.

"Better, ear." She leaned forward with ease. First, her stomach hit the floor, then she smiled and turned her head, gently placing her ear to the indoor/outdoor carpeting.

He shifted. Things just got way out of control south of the border.

She rolled her inner thighs across the carpet, making it look easy until she lay in front of him on her stomach, her feet in the air, ankles crossed. She had the biggest, sexiest smile across her face. "I studied ballet for years. Kind of my way to deal with life."

"Well, it sure paid off." He tossed what was left of his beer back, finishing it in one giant gulp. Now he felt good and buzzed, but it did nothing for the big fella. He wanted to come out and dance. With her.

"Can I ask you a question?" She sat up, inching a little closer to him.

"Shoot." He took her wine glass and sipped.

"Are you good in bed?"

He spit the wine out as he coughed and choked. She couldn't have just asked him if he was good in the sack. "What?" he managed moments later, still coughing.

"You heard me," she said tersely, fiddling with her toe ring.

"I don't know." How did one answer that? "I mean, no one's ever complained." Now he sounded like an ass. "Why?" He lifted her chin with this thumb.

She quickly took the wine glass and finished it in

one swallow. "My experiences have really sucked, and I've pretty much given up on the idea of ever liking sex." She looked everywhere but at him.

"You don't like it because of…" He couldn't form the words.

"I'm sure the rape has something to do with it, but I'm not afraid of sex. My therapist thinks it has more to do with my inability to connect with people. She says I spend too much time focusing on my career and not enough on myself and forming meaningful relationships."

"Your therapist is probably right."

"Are you speaking from experience?"

"My entire family thinks I spend too much time on my career. They are constantly trying to fix me up."

"I know."

"Wonderful," Travis said. "Was it just my mother, or was the rest of the family involved?"

She laughed. "Mostly your mom. She actually asked if agents were allowed to date."

"She's bound and determined to find me the right woman."

"She loves you."

"Yeah. She does." Travis took another sip of his wine. "My turn to ask a personal question."

"Okay."

"What was your first sexual experience like?"

"Unfortunately, it was the rape."

"I'm sorry."

"It took me a long time to get past it. I met this guy in college and I really liked him, but I couldn't bring myself to tell him about the rape. I thought it might wig him out or something."

"What happened?"

"He noticed how much I didn't enjoy being with him and took it personally, ending the relationship."

"Did you ever try to talk to him about it after?"

"No. I figured I needed more time in therapy. Then I got this bright idea to pick up a guy in a bar and just do it. I still didn't like it. Not sure he did either."

"I imagine rape would be a hard thing to get over."

"My therapist told me I needed to tell my partners, so my last boyfriend knew all about the rape, and I really thought he understood."

He moved closer to her, then leaned his back against the railing and drew her between his legs. Slicking back her hair, he rested his chin on the top of her head and wrapped his arms around her. "What didn't he understand?"

"Me, I guess. He couldn't…I couldn't…I mean, well, things had started to heat up in the bedroom, but it wasn't enough for him, I guess."

"Had you started to enjoy lovemaking?"

"Certain aspects of it, yes."

"So what happened?"

"He decided to get it elsewhere with a woman who could fake multiple orgasms better than I could." Her voice sounded less hurt and more angry. Somehow it made him feel better.

"You shouldn't have to fake anything."

"I only tried to fake it with him because he would get so mad and frustrated because he couldn't make me...I was never able to, umm...well..." she paused, taking a deep breath, "I thought it would make him feel better. I guess you'd need to have one, to know how to fake one." She pulled away from Travis and turned. "I get the impression you're the kind of lover who would be...considerate, figure out what worked, or didn't."

Floored by the conversation, he stared at her for a moment. "I have my moments, but I can be a selfish bastard."

"I just thought—"

"Don't," he snapped.

Her gaze met his. "You understand so much more than most men. You make me want...I feel...like a woman when I'm with you." Her hand moved to his thigh.

"I'm flattered, but you can't be suggesting that you and I, that we...?" He let the words hang.

She nodded.

"We'd lose our jobs." He swallowed, wanting her more than anything, and she was offering herself to him.

"No one would ever know but us. Besides, you've already kissed me. That alone could get you fired." She pursed her lips.

Hell, he'd initiated the kiss; she was right. He could get canned if anyone found out. At most, she'd get scolded. Sleeping with her would not only be detrimental to his career, it would put an end to the never-ending pool of information he needed to find his sister's killer. "You can't be serious?" He heard his voice crack.

She stood, placing her hands on the railing, and looked out over the bay. "Do you have any idea what it's like to live like this? I had been content to think that sex sucked. Then, *bam*, you come along, stirring all these feelings inside me, making me think that things could be different. God, Travis, I don't understand. No one has ever made me feel this way before." She closed her eyes.

Travis rose on shaky legs. "Shauna, look at me." He wanted nothing more than to take her in his arms and show her what making love could be like. He wasn't sure he could give her everything she wanted, but he was confident she would, at the very least, like it...a little.

But he couldn't. It wouldn't be right. Damn his conscience. "Open your eyes, sweetheart."

He heard her suck in a breath as her eyelids fluttered open. The blue of her eyes flickered in the starlight that rippled against the lake. Being a gentleman had never been harder.

"I think I've had too much to drink." She tried to look away, but he wouldn't let her.

"Believe me. It's not that I don't want to." He pulled her close, pressing his erection against her. "I want you." He couldn't resist kissing her, but he kept the kiss under control, ending it long before he wanted to.

She cupped his face and pulled him back to her mouth. Her tongue felt hot and wet against his lips.

"Shauna." He tried desperately to maintain control as he gripped her hips. Abruptly, he pushed her back.

Sadness filled her eyes.

"Do you have any idea what you're doing to me?" His breath came in short pants, and his pulse quickened with each breath.

"I suspect the same thing you do to me," she answered softly.

He traced her bottom lip and then nipped it with his teeth. "I want to be with you. I have since I saw you at the airport." He pressed his mouth against hers, parting her lips and tasting her sweet tongue. Her lips molded against his as if they were two pieces of a puzzle.

When he thought he might die a happy man, he pulled away. Searching her eyes for some kind of understanding, he brushed a tear away from her cheek. "Not like this," he whispered.

"Please, Travis."

Tormented, his mind shifted between his desire for her and his desire to do right by her. Part of him wanted to just take her and chalk it up to meaningless sex.

But she wasn't meaningless. She was the kind of woman he could be with. She was the kind of woman he would want to find after he put Marie's killer away for good. Why did she have to come into his life… now…under these circumstances? *Everything happens for a reason.*

"No," he said softly against her cheek.

She pulled away from him as if she had been slapped, then she ran from the deck.

"Real smooth." He grabbed the wine glass and empty beer bottle and headed for the house.

Rinsing out the empty glass, he stared out at the stillness of the night, listening to the water gently roll against the shore. He couldn't let things stay this way, and he wasn't going to wait until morning. He had to make her understand that he couldn't risk it, not now.

Closing the bedroom door, Shauna stood and looked around the room. She could smell his mixture of aftershave and sex appeal everywhere. "Damn him." She threw herself on the bed face down and cried.

How could she suggest that they sleep together? He was her partner, her mentor. Being attracted to each other meant nothing. Was she so desperate to feel like a woman that she would throw herself at the first decent man who showed her any interest?

No. She leapt from the bed and smoothed out her shirt. She needed to sleep off the effects of the alcohol and then stay away from it—and Travis. Not necessarily in that order.

She pulled her shirt over her head and heard a noise behind her.

"Shauna, I—" Travis said.

Turning, she gasped as she struggled to cover herself, and then she dropped her shirt to the floor.

He was in her room, and he was staring at her. He said nothing, just looked at her. His piercing gaze burned her body with pure heat. She could do nothing but drop her hands to her sides and hold her breath.

In less than a second, he moved across the room, and his mouth was on hers. His tongue parted her lips and brushed over her teeth. The intention, when her hands touched his shoulders, was to push him away. She couldn't handle another rejection. But when she felt the heat that echoed her own, she opened her mouth for his tongue and clasped her fingers behind his neck.

His strong hands pressed against her bare back, sending electric pulses throughout her body. She arched against his chest.

Her lips felt cold when he moved his kisses to her cheek. His moist tongue glided across her ear, sending wonderful goose bumps down her spine. She could barely catch her breath as he traced a path with his index finger down her neck. His lips followed, applying just enough pressure against her skin. She caved to her deepest desires, letting herself feel him. Only him.

No longer in control, Shauna had to touch his skin. Feel his nakedness against her fingers. She tugged at his shirt.

He must have felt her frustration because he whipped his shirt off so fast she barely had time to realize his lips had left her body.

When he cupped her breast, she gasped. She hadn't expected it to feel so intimate. It was like he released her, allowing her to feel what she had been missing most of her life. She felt a connection with him like no other person she had ever known.

His lips danced about her neck, while his fingers did things to her nipple that sent her into a world she didn't know existed. Her whole body warmed and throbbed for him.

Taking in a deep breath, she offered her breasts to his mouth. Much to her delight, his tongue circled her nipple, teasing her in such a way she thought she might die.

She held his head in her hands as he drew her nipple all the way into his mouth.

"Oh, Travis," she whispered, feeling his tongue glide under her breast. She looked down at him as he moved to his knees, his tongue circling her belly button. His hands dug into her backside, leaving behind his fingerprints.

A slight jolt of reality hit her when he pulled her jeans down over her hips, down her thighs, and encouraged her to step out of them. "What are you doing?"

Still on his knees, he looked up at her, his eyes hazy with passion, lust, desire, or all three. "Giving you pleasure." He kissed her stomach, his fingers curling in the lace of her panties. His steamy breath was moist against her sex, making her hotter than she thought was possible.

Her body shuddered. He gave her pleasure, all right.

She brought her hands to his head, wanting to run her fingers through his hair.

"Go ahead." He looked up at her.

Tentatively, she threaded her fingers through this thick, dark hair. It was soft and full and perfect. She could feel him chuckle against her skin.

"Oh, my. Ohhh. I—" Her head dropped back as he eased her panties down her legs. He kissed his way up her thigh to her hipbone and then across her stomach. "I'm scared," she said, barely audible.

"Don't be. If you don't like this, tell me. I can stop anytime," he said softly before she felt him kiss her in the most intimate way a man could.

"You're so beautiful." He slipped his fingers between her legs, slowly entering her. When she looked down, she gasped, surprised to see him looking so intently at her, at what he was doing to her.

Her breathing tightened, and her pulse raced with need. Running her fingers through his hair, she encouraged him to kiss her again.

"I want you to lie down." He eased her back onto the bed, lifting her knees. "Are you okay?"

She nodded, unable to speak.

"Relax." His fingers glided inside her while he kissed her swollen nub. Afraid she might scream, she bit down on her lower lip. Her body tensed as she felt a wave of instant pleasure wash through her, but then it was gone.

He looked up at her. "Shauna, sweetheart. Are you okay?"

She breathed unevenly but managed to nod again.

"Do you like this?"

"Yes." She moaned. "Please," she heard herself beg as her body began to shiver under his gentle touch. She relaxed and knew she would find heaven. It was right there for her to discover, seek, and savor. She wanted it.

He caressed and kissed her in ways no one could describe. His touch sent electric pulses to every inch of her body. "Oh, Travis," she cried as her body reached its limit, convulsing with his movements.

He stilled for a few moments before he lay next to her, studying her face.

"Travis, I…I never… Oh, God, I had no idea."

"We're not done yet." He smiled, scooting from the bed and stood before her. "That was just a preview."

"It gets better?" She smiled.

"God, I hope so." He undid his belt buckle, sliding the long, black belt from its loops.

She watched him undress, amazed she wasn't the least bit embarrassed, until he removed his boxers. Still, she wasn't afraid, not with him. Her senses electrified in anticipation. Seeing him naked only made her want him more.

"You're gorgeous," he said tenderly.

She moved to her knees, throwing her arms around his shoulders. "So are you." She kissed him for the first time with feverish intent. She felt a sudden surge of empowerment.

He cupped her face and looked deep into her eyes. "I saw your pills. If you want, I can still use a condom, but I'd rather not."

"Do I need to be worried?" She knew all the dangers of sex. She also knew she hadn't taken the last few pills in this current pack. She didn't take them regularly. She didn't know why she kept them.

"It's been a really long time, and no. You don't need to worry." Just as the words left his mouth, his tongue sought hers, cutting off her ability to speak, much less think.

She had meant to tell him to use the condom, but she couldn't. The heat his mouth offered was too sweet, and she wanted to feel him inside her, without any barriers.

She had enough barriers in her life.

He eased her onto her back, nudging her legs apart. She felt his hardness against her. "Anything you don't like, or don't want me to do, or if you want to stop, just tell me. Okay?" He kissed her nose.

This man was just too good to be true. "Who are you? And where did you come from?" She cupped his face, searching for answers.

"I'm just a man." His words were soft and sensitive, but she somehow felt he wasn't being humble. He didn't see himself as anything out of the ordinary, but he was unique, special.

"You're more than a man, Travis. Make love to me."

"Not to you, *with* you." He pushed down, slowly.

Arching her back, she accepted his length inside her. "Travis," she whispered.

"Shauna," he answered, moving in strong but

gentle strokes inside her. He kissed her lips, her neck, her breasts.

She wiggled underneath him. Her body now knew the pleasure he could bring her, and she demanded it.

"It's okay if it doesn't happen again," he said as if he could feel her frustration.

"But I want it to. I want to come with you," she said boldly, cupping his face.

"Roll over on top of me." He gripped her hips and pushed them back and forth over him. He lifted his head and brought his tongue to her nipple.

She felt closer, but it wasn't until he touched her where their bodies were joined together that she felt a second wave of passion, stronger than the first one, shocking her.

Just when she thought her body was done, she felt his release deep inside her as he called out her name in a grunt.

"Oh, God." She ground her hips hard back and forth as her body quivered violently. The intensity of her emotions, coupled with the fierce physical contact, sent her system into overdrive.

No longer in control, she released the tears fighting to be free.

"Shh. It's okay." He gripped her hips, slowing her down, pulling her close to him. "Shh, sweetheart." His fingers tangled through her hair as he soothed away the raw emotion that rocked her body.

She didn't know how long she cried, but when she

took a big cleansing breath, she was on her side, pulled close to him, and he was still whispering sweet, loving words in her ears. "I had no idea." She sighed.

"I should've been more careful with you."

When she looked at him, his eyes looked so damned caring. She had to force the tears away since she didn't want to start again. "You were wonderful."

"It was too intense. I should've known and been more gentle." He propped up on one elbow, while his other hand rubbed up and down her arm.

"If that wasn't gentle, then I think I might like to see your idea of rough."

That earned a laugh.

"Will you stay with me?" She closed her eyes, snuggling against his hard body.

"Do you want me to?"

She nodded.

"Shauna, you understand that this can't happen again. Even if we want it to. I don't want to tarnish your reputation. You're too good an agent to be tainted by something like this. Besides, I don't want to lose my job. It's my life, what I live for."

For the first time, his voice sounded almost demanding. He wasn't giving her a choice. But she understood. While she didn't regret making love with him, she did regret that it would never happen again. She regretted even more that someday he would hate her for lying to him.

"Shauna?" He gave her a questioning glance.

"I understand. I don't want to lose my job either. Can we just have tonight? I don't want to be alone right now." She tried not to sound like she was pleading. She would feel empty if he left her. Like it meant nothing to him.

"If the circumstances were different, I would want to take you out to the movies, kiss you goodnight, and pray like hell you would invite me into your room."

"Thank you."

"I mean——"

She covered his mouth. She didn't want to know if he really wanted more or not. He was willing to give her one night. That would have to be enough. "We could make love again." She smiled, hopefully seductively.

"God, you're sexy." He smiled wickedly.

It made her dizzy with anticipation.

"Inviting me into your room?" he teased.

"Just for tonight." She would let him take her as many times as he wanted tonight. She knew when she woke in the morning, it would be over.

"Maybe if we don't sleep, tomorrow will never come," he said, right before he kissed her passionately with a promise of pure pleasure.

Afterward, when she curled up in his arms, she let herself feel for the first time in her life. She felt like a woman, a woman who loved and had loved back. She felt whole, and at the same time, empty. Empty because her secret would destroy her life. Again.

9

Travis lay on his back, holding Shauna as close as he could. Even with the sun trying to push its way into the bedroom, he wanted to savor the feeling her body gave to him for as long as he could. Being with her made him realize he hadn't been living at all, but merely existing. The tenderness of her soul had awakened him.

Sex hadn't meant much to him, just a need that he satisfied on occasion. It was like wine. He could take it or leave it. Until now. He had made love to her more times last night than he'd had sex over the last two years.

The connection he had with her was so strong that breaking it would be like losing another part of himself. Turning to look at the angel who lay beside him, his heart pounded in pain. He hadn't wanted to care again.

At first he thought it was because he had given her body satisfaction. He made her feel desirable, like a woman should, but she was more than just desirable. She was damn likable, too. When he made love with her the second time, she gave her whole self. There was no hesitation, no fear of the unknown, just pure, uninhibited lovemaking that sucked up his senses. He had to make love with her again. If only to make sure he wasn't dreaming.

She stirred.

She stirred him.

"Hi." She cleared her throat, running her fingers across his chest.

Taking her hand, kissing her palm, he tried to ease the tightness in his throat. She smiled at him with a morning glow that sucker-punched his ability to think.

"Screw it," he muttered, taking her mouth with his. It was Saturday, and while they were still technically on the job, it was the weekend. Unless they got called, they weren't punching a time clock. Therefore, he would take the weekend.

The whole damned weekend.

"What are you doing?" He tugged a little too harshly at her hair while she gently nipped at his nipples. She stroked him, teasing him, slowly pushing him over the edge.

"Giving you pleasure." Her voice was as alluring as her smile. She nipped at his nipple again.

Closing his eyes, he grunted. She gripped him, and he groaned again. She was going to kill him.

Then she tortured him by taking her bites down his stomach. He sucked in a sharp breath. She hadn't done this last night, and he would never have asked. Had she not been so damn good at touching him, he would have felt like a guinea pig.

She held him in her hands, admiring him, stroking him, basically driving him insane. He could feel her breath on him. All he wanted to do was reach down and push himself into the warmth of her mouth, but he gripped the sheets instead, forcing his body to stay in control.

First her tongue flicked out and touched him. He hissed, looking at the erotic position she was in, hovering over him. Dizzy, he dropped his head back on the pillow as she took him in her hot mouth.

Not having much control left, he reached down and ran his fingers through her hair, trying desperately not to lose it. "Come here," he demanded, pulling her by the hair. "Sorry." He blinked, forcing himself to calm down.

She sat next to him on her heels, smiling. "Don't be. You've held back every time. I don't want you to."

He sat up, cupping her face and kissing her swollen lips.

"Tell me how you want me." Her eyes told him she wanted it all.

God, he wanted her so much it hurt.

"Like this." He placed her hands on the bed, turning her, lifting her hips to him as he stood. He rubbed her behind, her back, then frowned as his finger glided across a scar. Feeling the need to soothe her skin with his touch, he bent over and kissed the whitish line across the arch of her back, then his fingers found her wetness, and her legs spread in acceptance.

She looked over her shoulder. Her gaze blazed, like a passionate woman wanting to give her lover everything he gave to her.

Slowly he entered her, feeling her tightness around him. He wouldn't last but a few minutes. He held her still, leaning over her and wrapping his arms around her. He pulled at her aroused nipples as she tried to move him inside her. He couldn't, not yet.

He wanted to give first. "Stay still." He bit down on her back.

"I can't," she cried, still wiggling.

He chuckled. She was so close. Giving up trying to make it last, he caressed her where their bodies merged while his other hand reached across her chest, managing to excite both nipples at the same time. He still didn't drive himself inside her. He wanted to feel her release around him.

"Oh, God," she cried out, pushing against him.

"Shauna." He grunted. Her orgasm rushed over

him again and again. Seconds later, he pushed her hips hard against his and held her there. Neither one breathed for what seemed like an eternity.

"Are you okay?" he asked, gliding her down on her stomach when he could finally breathe. He lay next to her, propped up on his elbow.

Her smile said it all.

Her kiss said it better. "Always the gentleman," she teased him.

He cocked a brow. "That wasn't very gentlemanlike."

"It wasn't very ladylike either." Her smile turned wicked.

He frowned, rubbing her back. He had one question that had to be answered. "What happened here?" The scar looked almost like a whip's mark, but at the end it appeared to be indented, almost like a chunk had been taken from her side about the size of a half dollar.

He shifted his gaze from her scar to her face. "The rape?"

"No."

"Then who did this to you?" He tried to keep his voice even. It hadn't occurred to him until just that moment that someone had done this intentionally. "Tell me." He felt his control snap.

Shauna took a deep breath, knowing that this conversation had been inevitable. "My stepmother pushed me through a glass window. It was a clean cut for the most part. She kicked me here." She reached to her side and rubbed the knotted scar. "A piece of glass was lodged there. It was hours before my father got me to a hospital, and it had already gotten infected." All this was true, but she left out that it was a scar on top of a scar. What her stepmother had done had been a blessing in disguise. The branding would now forever be gone.

Shauna saw the tension in his face. She could feel his contempt. "Where's your stepmother now?" His jaw grew rigid, but his touch across her back felt tender and soothed her pain.

"I don't know, and I don't give a shit." Oh, she knew, but she didn't care.

"I give a shit."

"Let it go. She's an unhappy woman, living a nightmare. She's getting worse than what she deserves. Last I heard, she was dying." She stood, taking his boxers and pulling his shirt over her head. She needed to end the conversation. She didn't want to think about Roxanne or her father. She never wanted to see either one of them again.

"How can you just forgive them?"

"It's not worth carrying anger and sadness like that around. It just bogs you down. I don't want to live in the past. Can you understand? I need to keep moving forward. I've got a lot going for me." She meant every word that spewed from her mouth. It wasn't just fluff, but it had taken her years to believe the words. She knew it wouldn't take much to bring her confidence down, which is why she chose to focus her energies on her career.

"Those belong to me." He tugged at the boxers, trying to pull them down and redirect the conversation.

She pushed him back on the bed, shaking her finger at him. "I earned the right to wear these this morning." She laughed. "Want coffee?" She turned, hearing him grunt a yes as she headed out of the bedroom to find the coffeemaker, but just as she turned the corner, she came in contact with a large moving object.

"Oh, crud! Sorry." Shauna put her hand on the back of Travis's brother, Bill. He hunched over, not breathing all too well from the belt she had given to his stomach. "I didn't know who you were. It was a knee-jerk reaction." She shook out her hand. "Damn, you're built like a tree trunk."

"Damn good reaction." Bill coughed. "Mac truck, actually."

Shauna glanced over her shoulder and saw Travis hiking up his zipper. She glanced back at Bill, who arched a brow. She knew her perfect night had to come to an end, but she hadn't expected it to come to an end by getting caught.

"Jess is——"

"Standing right behind you, Dad. Real smooth, Uncle Trav. Nice hit, Miss Morgan." The teenager giggled.

Shauna looked over Bill's shoulder. Jessica had turned and headed back down the hallway.

"Great. Another conversation in sex ed," Bill said.

"What the hell are you doing here?" Travis asked.

"Watering Mother's plants." Bill glared at Travis. "Hi, Shauna."

"Hi."

"Didn't Mom tell you I was coming?"

Bill shook his head.

"What? Missed the truck parked in the driveway?" Travis raked his hand through his hair.

"Boat."

"Excuse me." Shauna dodged Bill and eased her way toward the kitchen. She could still hear their muffled voices, each sounding angry with the other. She really didn't feel like standing in the middle of it since she seemed to be the cause it. Jessica followed her.

"You made coffee." Shauna smelled the hint of hazelnut in the air before she heard the coffeemaker gurgle. She watched it drip, hoping that it would go faster with an audience. It seemed to go slower.

"I guess you really like my uncle, huh?" Jessica spoke quietly.

Shauna looked at the teenager and wanted to laugh. She had a protective glare shimmering in her eyes. Shauna's own embarrassment left the building. But how did she answer that?

"I do." What the heck, she did. Even if she hadn't slept with him, she still liked him. She would never be able to deny that.

"Grandma thinks you're the perfect woman for him."

Shauna spilled the hot coffee on her hand as she poured it. "Damn it."

"Grandma usually gets her way."

"Huh?" Shauna turned.

"My grandmother, she has this weird ability to make people see things her way. She said the next time she saw the two of you, she would start to weave her magic, just like she did with my parents." The teenager didn't smile but seemed to study Shauna. "I might agree with my grandmother. I like you. Couldn't you get fired for…" Her face flushed bright pink as she waved her arms in the air.

Shauna had to admire the girl's spunk, but she suspected her own cheeks were as red as they were warm. "Fired is putting it mildly." Shauna heard the voices getting louder. Either the argument was getting out of control, or they were coming toward the kitchen. "Come on." She pulled Jessica by the arm, and they both headed down to the lake.

Once perched on the edge of the dock with feet dangling in the water, Shauna decided to pump Jessica for info she had no business looking into. But she couldn't resist.

"So, Jessica. Tell me about your uncle's other girlfriends." Shauna sipped her coffee. She had gone from feeling like a woman to a stupid teenager in just a few seconds.

"Does that mean you're his girlfriend?" Jessica's voice rang out in excitement as she kicked the water.

"No."

"Oh."

Shauna felt the disappointment that echoed in her ears from Jessica's simple response. "The job." It was the job—at least for Travis—that would keep them apart. For Shauna, it was a whole lot more.

"I've never met any of his other girlfriends. Well, except the ex-yucky Gina we never talk about."

Shauna's heart stopped, then picked up speed as soon as she let herself breathe. She blew on her hot coffee, trying to decide how to process this information. "Why is that?" Shauna heard herself ask.

"He hasn't dated much since he and Gina split. My dad says he's obsessed with trying to find my aunt's killer—that it drives him." Jessica continued to splash her feet in the cool lake water.

"It does."

"My mom says he's been hurt and doesn't trust women much. I think he trusts you."

Shauna took another sip of her coffee, looking out across the lake. If that were true, she didn't deserve his trust.

"I look like her," Jessica said softly.

Shauna turned to her. Tears had formed in the young girl's eyes. Shauna smoothed Jessica's long, black hair. "You do."

"I'm about her age. Sometimes I worry that the killer will think I'm her and come after me." She sniffled.

"Your uncle and I are going catch him and make sure he pays for what he did." She hadn't meant to sound so serious, but she could understand Jessica's fear. She always felt like the killer was out there, watching, waiting for her to come back to him.

Jessica threw her arms around Shauna and cried.

Shauna put her coffee mug down and held Jess. "What is it?" She stroked her hair.

"I don't even remember her. I was just a baby when she died. No one talks about her with me because they think it upsets me. But what really gets me is they always stop talking when I come into the room. I'm not a baby." She lifted her head.

Shauna saw so much emotion in such a young girl. "They're doing what they think is best for you. That's all." Hearing the crackle of gravel, Shauna turned and looked over her shoulder to see Bill jogging down the path.

Jessica swiped her tears from her face. "Please don't tell my dad I was talking to you about all this."

"All right."

"Come on, pumpkin." Bill took his daughter by the hand and helped her onto the boat. "Start her up," he called as he helped Shauna to her feet and guided her away from the dock. He looked at Jessica before turning his attention back to Shauna.

"That fight had nothing to do with you," he said right after the boat engine came to life.

She figured the fight had been about a lot of things, including her.

"Travis has my wife all wigged out about Marie's killer. While I believe everything my brother says, I don't want my family scared shitless." His eyes looked like he was carrying the burden of the world in them.

"This may be overstepping my bounds, but talk to Jessica about Marie. She knows how much she looks like her. She's scared all on her own, and she wants to know about her aunt. She needs to hear from you that it's okay to be scared, but not to let it run her life. Just to be safe."

"She told you this?" His brow lifted.

"I shouldn't say anything. She doesn't want you to know."

"She doesn't talk much to us these days. She's a

good kid, gets good grades, but she's starting to rebel. Frankly, that scares me."

"She's not Marie."

He tilted his head and smiled. "Shauna Morgan, quit your job so my brother can keep you."

Before she had a chance to close her mouth and say something other than a grunt, he jumped on the boat and then coaxed his daughter to drive away.

Jessica turned and waved.

Shauna felt the tears hit the back of her eyes. She waved, taking in deep breaths. Travis was a lucky man to have such a wonderful family. They were all lucky.

She ran her fingers across the indentation in her back. Standing on the dock, she watched the wake behind the boat. She felt like the waves—rolling around, waiting to crash against the shore, just to be sent back out to hit the other side.

The question remained: when would she hit the other side, and how much would it hurt?

She looked up to see Travis standing on the front deck, hair mussed, jeans still partly undone.

"Not today," she muttered to herself, heading up the path. The crash against the shore would have to wait.

Travis wanted to make sure his family remained safe from a ruthless killer. His gut told him the bastard was still lurking in the shadows. Travis always trusted his instincts, except when it came to women. He had been wrong about Gina, so wrong. But he wasn't wrong about Shauna. She was keeping something from him. Something important about Jane Doe.

He scowled.

"What's wrong?" Shauna asked as she glided up the stairs to the deck.

The feel of her fingers against his scalp as she ran them through his hair made him want to forget she was lying to him about something.

He grabbed her wrist. "Stop."

Her eyes narrowed. "What crawled up your butt?"

"What do you know about Marie's case that you're not telling me?" He held her wrist tighter than he should have.

His phone beeped.

He released her to pick up his cell. "It's Scott." He turned from her, not wanting to see the hurt he had put on her face. "Hi, Scott. What's up?" Travis stared out over the lake.

"Another body, but this time the locals picked up a suspect. I need you here right away. Any idea where Shauna is?"

Travis rubbed his jaw; he was going to have to lie to his boss. "Yeah, I can reach her. I need an hour and half or so; I'm at my parents'." He turned to Shauna, who didn't look much better than he felt.

"You do that, get here ASAP," Scott barked as if

he'd picked up on the fact Travis had been staring into her eyes.

Travis took down the information Scott gave him. Moments after he hung up, Shauna's cell phone rang out. "Shit. Answer it. I'll be in the shower." Travis wondered if he would even get through the next few hours without getting fired.

He didn't hang out to hear her conversation with Scott. One thing he knew for sure: Shauna wanted this bastard as bad as he did.

The drive to Albany had been silent. Shauna didn't even look at him. Pulling into the police station, Travis decided to open his mouth. "I won't blow this. What happened at my parents', stays at my parents'." He jerked the car into park and turned.

"Get over yourself," she said in a huff, not waiting for him to open the door.

"Shauna."

She looked over her shoulder. "We've got a job to do," she snapped, picking up the pace and heading for the door. "Let's do it."

He'd be damned if he was going to let her get to him. He smiled, opening the door for her.

"Thank you."

A sudden chill hit his bones with her clipped tone, but he had to let it go.

They were greeted by two police officers who took them down to the two-way room. Once inside, they were given an update on the latest victim who was found in a dumpy hotel in downtown Albany. The Princess Killer had struck again.

Travis held the note the killer had left behind. It was basically the same, saying he was right there, watching, and warned that some people weren't who they said they were. This time he knew it came from one of Shauna's journals. He knew this because on the back was her handwriting. It was smudged and some of the words were crossed out, but it was Shauna's. The look on her face confirmed it.

"What do you make of the note?" Scott asked.

"A game. He's rubbing our face in it. For whatever reason, he's snapped." Travis cracked his neck. The tension was killing him. "Who is this guy?" Travis pointed to the man who was sitting alone in the room behind the two-way mirror.

"We found him with this, two doors down." A detective who Travis didn't know, held up one of Shauna's journals.

Travis glanced at Shauna. She stood still and tall. He didn't want to be impressed by her ability to carry herself in this situation, but he had to be. "Do we know who it belongs to?" Travis looked around the room.

"Me." Shauna reached out and took the journal. "I left most of my journals with my dad, whom I haven't spoken to in years." She flipped through the pages. "I think I must have been about fifteen when I wrote in this one." Shauna tossed the book on the table, planted her hands on her hips, and didn't once look at Travis.

He prayed it had been left at her parents', and not one of the journals that had been stolen from her hotel. They'd never filed a report. Never told a soul. That would be enough to not only pull them from this case, but also to fire his ass.

"We fingerprinted it." Scott gave a pointed look at Travis. "This is too close for comfort."

"Tell me about it." Shauna stood facing the suspect. "This guy is toying with us," she added.

"Ya don't say," Travis muttered.

"How do you suspect he got your journal?" one of the policemen barked.

"Beats me. When I left home, I never looked back. Wait." She moved to the mirror, squinting. "Holy shit. Un-freaking believable." She ran a hand through her hair, and for the first time she looked at Travis. Her face had paled.

Travis didn't like this one bit. "What?" He moved to stand next to her.

"I know him. He was one of my brother's friends in school. A known drug dealer back then. He also had a little fondling problem. I think he got caught hiding in the girls' locker room."

"He's got a rap sheet a half-mile long. Been picked up for masturbating in public, peeping tom, and flashing," one of the cops said.

"Doesn't make for a rapist." Travis cracked his neck again.

"Might explain how he got your journals, though," Scott said under his breath.

"I doubt he's our guy, but he knows something." She turned. "I want to talk to him," she said, placing her hands on her hips, the color coming back to her cheeks.

"Works for me," Scott said.

"Will he recognize you?" Travis tried to hide his concern. He was crossing the line from FBI Agent to caring man. Not very comfortable in a room full of cops.

"I hope so," she said, glancing over her shoulder as she left.

Travis stood in front of the mirror, eyeing the suspect. This sicko would be alone with Shauna. He could do something, and it would take at least three minutes before Travis could get to her. That made him sick to his stomach.

Shauna took a deep breath, gripping the door handle to the interrogation room. Chester Wilson was a pervert, no doubt. But he wasn't her rapist. Blinking, she tried to remember everything she could. The wig, the blond hair under the wig and the Yankees baseball cap, but she couldn't see her attacker's face.

It was blocked from her memory. She pushed open the door.

"Hello, Chester." She kept her back stiff and her voice strong. No one was going to rattle her today, except maybe Travis. But he did that every day. Her eyes darted to the mirror.

"Shauna Morgan?" Chester's chin dropped to the floor, and his eyes bulged.

"*Agent* Morgan. Tell me how you got this?" She tossed the journal on the table.

He smiled. It was an eerie smile, and it made the hair on her arms stand up. Not much different than when she knew him in high school.

"I found it next to the dead body."

"Why'd you kill her? Not really your style." Shauna sat across from him. Her heart was pounding, and she forced her hands still. "You like to look, but that's about it."

"I didn't kill her. She was dead when I found her."

"But you didn't call the cops."

"Nope, don't like them." He frowned and looked toward the mirror. "Knew they would try to pin this on me."

"If so, why stick around?" Shauna flipped through her journal, pages were missing, words crossed out. It was like he was taking pieces of her away, little by little, until she would no longer exist.

Chester leaned forward, smiling that smug, sadistic smile he had. "Because I would look guilty if I ran." His hand was on his lap. "I have something I'd like to show you, Shauna. Do you remember?" His finger tapped at her knee.

"Touch me again, asshole, and I will slam your face against the wall." She looked deep into his eyes. He wasn't The Princess Killer. He wasn't old enough, and his hair was the wrong color. She leaned closer. "Where did you get the journal?"

"I found it in the dead girl's hotel room." He sneered, gripping her leg, while he reached into his pants.

"I warned you."

Just as the door opened, she grabbed his wrist, twisting it, and pulling him to a standing position.

"Shauna." Travis entered the room. But he was too late.

Shauna slammed Chester against the mirror. "Keep your dick in your pants and your hands to yourself, asshole." She gave him one last shove and then flew past Travis into the hallway where she ran right into Scott.

"You okay?" Scott took her by the shoulders.

"Just freaking great."

"I'm sorry. By the time we figured out what he was doing…well, you had it under control. Either way, we get to keep him for a while."

Shauna was grateful for that. She felt a warm prickle up her spine. She didn't have to turn around to know Travis had just placed his hand on her back. "He's not the Princess Killer," Shauna added.

"I agree, but how the hell did he get a childhood journal? And why?" Scott shot Travis a pointed glare that didn't go unnoticed by her. Shauna knew she had to explain this one, but not here.

"Can we talk outside?" She felt a little push by Travis, his way of agreeing.

Scott waved his hand out in front of them.

"Start talking," Scott demanded once they were outside.

Shauna didn't know quite where to start, or how to do this without downright lying. "When I was a teenager, I was raped."

"Tell me something I don't know." Scott raised a brow.

"You know all about my papers in school, don't you?"

Scott nodded. "Agent Rollings is a close friend."

"I've always kept journals." She scowled. Agent Rollings knew a lot about her past life, and he had done his best to help her through the programs at Quantico. He used to tell her to use her knowledge as a victim to help categorize the criminal. "The one Chester had, I had left at my parents' house, along with a few others. They have nothing to do with my ideas on serial rapists, just facts about my rape and what was going on when I was a kid. I started the journals after I started counseling." She took a breath, feeling Travis's entire body tighten.

She didn't know if she should be flattered or scared. The truth needed to come out, and if he wanted to hate her, well, that was his business. Nothing was going to stop her now.

"I graduated a year early and took off the same day, leaving everything behind. Knowing Roxanne, my stepmother, she would've had me arrested if I took even my own clothing."

"You implied there were other journals," Scott said, not hiding his frustration.

"I kept notes about my theories, other victims."

"Travis's sister?" Scott muttered.

"Those journals were stolen from my room a few days ago."

"Jesus," Travis muttered, hands on his hips, and it looked like he was trying not to pace.

"You knew about this?" Scott asked Travis.

"Not all of it, but...yeah, I knew." Lacing his fingers together, and then pressing his palms away from his body, he cracked every knuckle.

Shauna decided to give her own little theory a test spin. "Whoever this killer is, he knows about my past, knows about Travis's sister, and is using the fact we're working together to have his own little game of cat and mouse. It's like we gave him the opportunity to snap." She left out the fact the killer knew her because she was one of his victims.

"So let's catch this asshole before he makes us look bad." Scott pointed his finger at them. "You two are on thin ice. One complaint or problem, you are off the case—got it?"

Shauna and Travis nodded in unison. She knew they were lucky to still have their jobs, much less to be working on this case. Now she needed to find a way to feed information about what she was starting to remember to Travis, without telling him who she was. If he knew, she figured he would make damn sure she got fired. And shut her out completely.

She wouldn't let that happen until the Princess Killer was locked up. Or dead.

10

D ark gray clouds filled the night sky as a slight mist fell to the ground. The windshield wipers on Travis's truck swept back and forth, sloshing the water aside. He tried to concentrate on that instead of the mixed emotions embodied in his mind and soul.

When he'd watched Chester reach for himself and then touch Shauna, pure rage engulfed Travis. He'd wanted to strangle the bastard for touching what he, for one moment, had thought belonged to him. Blinded by his need to protect her, he'd bolted for the interrogation room, knocking into his boss and at least two other cops, who were completely capable of putting a stop to what had been happening in the other room.

The rest of the drive to his apartment had been chillingly silent. Shauna hadn't even glanced at him once. He, on the other hand, kept looking at her. He couldn't decide if he was proud of the way she'd handled herself, or angry with her.

There were too many coincidences for them to be truly coincidences. Either Special Agent Shauna Morgan knew who and where Jane Doe was.

Or she was Jane Doe.

Now well past nine, he sat on his couch, watching old sitcoms alone. Shauna had gone to bed right after dinner. They'd talked a little about nothing. He'd tried to get her to relax and open up. If she was Jane Doe, she'd have to know by now he was on her side. But she stayed clammed up all through dinner and then went off to her room, leaving him alone with his thoughts. He didn't like pondering, so he turned up the volume on the TV, but it didn't help. Regardless of who Shauna was, he still wanted her. That bugged the hell out of him.

"Travis?" Shauna's voice rang in his ears, soft and sweet.

"Hmm." He turned to see her standing in his kitchen, barefoot with his damned shirt and boxers on. "God, that's just way too sexy."

Letting out a breath, she said, "I need talk to you." She held a folder in her hands.

He didn't want to talk. He wanted to become ungentlemanly and rip his boxers off her. He stood and stared at her.

"I want—"

Watching her lips move, he had the undeniable

urge to touch them. Quickly, he hushed her with his finger.

"Talk later." The pink flesh of her mouth quivered as he glided his thumb across her lower lip.

She stared at him with a mixture of passion and fear. At present, his passion was painfully obvious.

Her eyes closed, and she leaned into his palm, taking his wrist in her hands. "We can't." A tear escaped her closed lids.

"Did Chester rape you?" He dropped his hand.

She shook her head and opened her eyes. "I wasn't raped in Saratoga, and it was a stranger." Her face tensed, and rage poured from her as she hit her hand against the wall. "Damn it! I can't remember his face. I couldn't remember enough to give the police anything to go on."

"What can you remember?" He kept his voice soft and calm. The last thing she needed was for him to lose control. Taking her by the hand, he led her to the sofa. "Tell me what you do remember."

"I wanted him to stop. I fought back, kicked him. But he just laughed at me." Her body stiffened. "I…I wish I knew something."

"They never caught him? Do you know if he raped others?" Travis controlled his breathing. Either he had another man to hunt down, or Jane Doe had found him.

"He fits the pattern of a serial rapist." She leaned back against the leather cushions.

Anger surged through Travis's veins, but surprisingly, he wasn't mad at her. Her hair felt soft against his fingers. He wanted desperately to take all her pain away. She had been through so much. She deserved to be loved and cherished. It killed him inside that it couldn't be him. "Are you trying to find him?" Roundabout way of asking, but he really wanted her to tell him.

She didn't answer.

"Shauna?" He pulled his hand away.

"What?"

He shook his head. "Nothing." No way. She couldn't be Jane Doe. Impossible. They were two completely unrelated cases. And she would have told him. Wouldn't she?

"What aren't you telling me?" A dull ache began to rise from his neck to his temples. She was driven by what happened to her and stumbled upon his sister's case. *Coincidence,* he chided himself.

"What I can't remember," she paused, and then said, "I want to see all the information you've gathered on all those girls taped to your ceiling and compare what I have in my paper on Matt Williams."

---

*S*hauna studied his thoughtful expression. He seemed to weigh her request, and it appeared he suspected her true identity. She should just tell him, but her body trembled with irrational fear. After everything his ex-girlfriend had put him through…the betrayal, Travis would never be able to forgive Shauna for lying to him.

"I'm scared, okay? This is personal for you, always has been. He just made it very personal for me. He's invaded my privacy." *In more ways than one.* Bile bubbled up toward her throat.

"Are you sure?" He cupped her face.

She took in a deep breath. "I don't know how to handle everything that's happened, but I want to nail this guy."

"So do I, but remember, this information is not official. Nothing about these files could be used by any legal system, not to mention, some of them I got by illegal means." He held her by the shoulders. "I'd get canned for sure."

"I think at this point, we're both on the edge." She followed him into his bedroom and glanced up at the ceiling. "Can I take them down?" The mattress squeaked as she climbed on the bed.

"I have another set in these files." He took out two home storage containers and started pulling out folders.

Swallowing hard, she sat on the bed and started looking at the names on each one. Unaware of his presence, she put them into piles, organizing them by date, crime scene, perceived virginity, leaving her file to the side.

She scanned all the official paperwork and then read Travis's notes. He had extensive notes.

Theories and ideas about who the girls were, why they ran away, who they were running from, and where he thought the killer might have picked them up.

Even though she didn't know these girls, she knew what happened to her, and Travis's instincts were right on the money. Grabbing a pen and a piece of paper, she added some of her own ideas. She kept facts out, things only a victim would know, but added what she called woman's intuition.

Finally, she picked up Jane Doe's file. She blinked, trying to make her body stop shaking. "Oh, God." A picture of her battered face shook in her hands.

"Sorry. I blew it up to try and match her face to any missing girls I could find." Travis snatched the picture away. "Whoever she is, no one reported her missing. You're amazing."

"Why?" Her heart pounded. She didn't feel amazing. She felt guilty, and responsible for all these girls. She felt like she'd let them down because she should have been able to figure out who the heck had killed them all.

"The way you break everything down and start from the beginning, ignoring the obvious. You look for what you can see but your eyes miss because it seems normal, or something you see all the time. You have instincts that can't be taught."

She'd never really thought about it. What she knew didn't come from instinct. It came from firsthand knowledge. She lifted her gaze to catch his. "Thanks."

"I mean it, Shauna. What you just did with these files took me years to put together this way. Not to mention this paper." He held it in his hands. "I'm impressed."

She gave him a half-smile, hoping he didn't see right through her. "You're not so bad yourself." The paper felt heavy in her hands as she skimmed through his file on her. Scary how good his instincts were. He had guessed she'd been approached at a train station or bus terminal.

It was the train station.

He assumed she hadn't been with the killer long, like some of the others. Maybe a couple of days.

It was only one night, but it had felt like a lifetime.

His notes stated he thought she might have fought back, where a lot of the other girls might have been passive.

She fought like hell after she'd come to, but it didn't stop him.

When the police had wanted to fingerprint her, she panicked. She took the first opportunity she saw and ran from those who were trying to help her. Barely able to see, her eyes beaten shut, she slipped out into the night and went home.

She thought about going to the police until she

saw on the news that they had captured her attacker, but when she heard him speak on the television, she knew they'd picked up the wrong guy. Going back meant the killer would find out her true identity. Not something she could live with at the time. She wasn't sure she could live with it now.

Travis wrote in his notes that he figured she was a runaway from a troubled home, possibly abused. He'd assumed that she had just walked right back into her old life, with no one the wiser.

Except him.

"You buyin' it?" he asked, sitting down next to her, collecting all the files.

She nodded, unable to speak. Guilt tore at her gut. But she couldn't tell him now. It would interfere with their investigation if he had to deal with her betrayal.

"I have a friend who puts facial structure back together on a computer. I was thinking about calling in a favor and having him do a composite on what she might look like now."

"How long would that take?" Her breathing became difficult. "What would you do with the picture?"

"Run it though our database, I guess."

The thought of her picture matching this one chilled her bones. "They wouldn't let you."

"Are you coming around to my way of thinking?"

"Tired of fighting you on this. How long?" she asked. Not that it mattered.

"Few days or so. Why are you so dead set against finding this woman?" His words were clipped.

"I understand her better than you think. Do you have any idea what it's like not knowing who tried to kill you? He put his hands on me…touched me…."

"Shauna," Travis said, taking a step closer to her.

Her hands shot up. "I never really saw his face, he hid it from me. The only thing I can remember for sure is his voice. I walk around constantly looking over my shoulder, wondering, worrying, listening."

"Why don't you go after him? I'll help you. I wouldn't mind wringing the bastard's neck personally." Travis snapped a pencil in half, with a deadly look on his face.

God, if he only knew.

"I thought about going after him, which is why I thought about going into police work in the first place, but between therapy and learning about the violent offenders, I realized it wasn't about him, as much as healing myself and helping others like me find peace, you know?"

"Yeah. I know," he said. "I find myself caring about you. I really don't want to." He stepped halfway into his closet, putting the files away.

"The feeling's mutual," she muttered, pacing about the bedroom. "Don't do that composite. Maybe she's been able to move past it."

"Like you have? Jesus, Shauna. You hide behind this strong woman, which you are. But you use it to protect yourself from the world. From your past. You're running around in circles, and you can't settle down because it's not finished yet. Sure, all that mumbo-jumbo you just spit at me is true, but that's only part of it. You won't rest until the bastard who hurt you is behind bars." The space between them narrowed until she'd backed herself into the wall.

"Look in the mirror before you go and analyze me," she shot back. "Talk about running in circles. You can't see straight. You're so obsessed with finding Marie's killer, you'd do anything, including using a young victim who wants to try to forget a nightmare. Add that to the fact you don't trust a single soul, even me—especially me. All because one woman broke your heart."

His mouth opened, but nothing came out.

"Take that." She turned and bolted across the kitchen to her bedroom, feeling quite satisfied. "Ugh." A firm grip snatched her arm, and then pulled her into his chest before he backed her into the wall inside her room. It hadn't been violent, but he held her firmly. Affection and desire seeped from every inch of his hard body.

"Do you have any idea what a turn-on it is when you get all riled up like that?" The heat radiating from his eyes burned her down to her core. "In every way, you amaze me." He traced her jawline with his knuckles.

"I could really mess with your manhood right now." She lifted her leg, applying pressure to his most sensitive area. The close physical contact would make it impossible to resist him.

His eyes closed as he inhaled sharply. "But you won't," he whispered, pressing his lips against her temple. "Tell me to stop." He moved his kisses to her lips. His mouth was hot and tasted of ginger ale. She welcomed his soft, probing tongue.

Cupping his face, she pushed his head from hers. "Kind of hard to talk when you do that."

He winked. "I told you earlier, I really don't want to talk."

"You're not as much of the gentleman you portray yourself to be," she teased him, wrapping her arms around his long, lean body. So much of her life had been temporary. Why should this be any different?

"Do you want me to stop?" He kissed her nose, her cheek, and then, with tender care, he brushed his lips across hers. "I never take."

"Unless offered," she said. Her words were barely audible.

"That wouldn't be taking. Besides, I saw what you're capable of. I think you could take me." His voice had a sense of challenge in it.

One she wasn't going to let go unnoticed.

"Really?" She kissed him, hard and wet. Just when she felt him relax from the shock of her kiss…

She let him have it.

First, she tripped him, making sure she landed on top of him. His eyes widened in surprise, then she flipped him over on his stomach with one arm twisted behind his back.

"Was that fun?" he asked, humor trickling from his voice.

"Loads."

"That's good."

Before she stopped giggling, he returned the favor, flipping her flat on her back, hands pinned high above her head. He lifted both brows.

"You think you've got me, don't you?" She smiled up at him, trying to catch her breath.

He waved his free hand as if he was swatting a fly. "Yep."

Lifting her legs, she tucked his head between her knees.

"Maybe not." His eyes shifted from side to side.

"Not!" She laughed, squeezing her knees together and pulling him toward the floor.

"That hurts," he said with a scowl.

"Then let go of my hands."

He did.

"Oh, you're done now." She tossed him onto his back, pinning him. "Well, now, that was almost as much fun as backing my stepmother's new car into the garage the day I left."

"You didn't." He tried to lift his hands, which were high above his head. "Damn, you're strong."

She rolled her eyes. "Thanks, but we both know you could get out of this if you really wanted to." She let go, still straddling him.

He grinned. "Why would I want to?" The muscles in her thighs relaxed as his strong hands massaged them into putty. "Come here." His voice was as smooth as hot honey dripping from a hive.

She should resist him. There were so many reasons why she should stand up and tell him to leave.

She dropped her lips to his and before she knew it, she was lying naked beneath him in a sea of emotion.

"Travis," she moaned, threading her fingers through his thick, dark hair.

He entered her in one slow, tender motion, never letting his gaze fall from hers. He traced his thumb across her cheek and then dipped his head to kiss her.

His lips sizzled against her tongue. Their bodies moved in perfect unison as if they were made for each other. The gentle touch of his hands tormented her body but filled her soul. She shuddered with release, and moments later, he whispered her name. He filled her in every way a man could, and she'd never felt so loved in her life.

But how could that be? He didn't love. She didn't

love. Yet here they were, tangled up in each other's web.

As the sun dipped into the room after a night of pure passion, Travis lay on his side, both hands tucked up under his cheek, and watched her sleep. She looked the most at peace when she slept. All her defenses were gone, and it was just her.

Her eyes fluttered open, and she stretched, catching him in her arms. "Good morning."

He fisted some of her hair and drew her lips close to his. "You're an amazing woman." Electricity mixed with the warm glow of fire filtered through his body when his lips brushed against hers.

"We're an amazing team." She smiled.

His reasoning took a flying leap as he told himself to get out of bed. Making love to her again would only compound the problems they were already facing. The other part of his body asked him what the heck difference did it make? They'd already made the mistake, why not enjoy it?

They spent the morning acting like a normal couple. They went for a run, showered, and had a leisurely breakfast, as if they could be together. He knew it would end again. It had to.

By the time he put the dishes away, awkwardness

had settled over them. "I have a lot of respect for you," Travis said. "I don't want to hurt you."

She leaned against the counter and crossed her arms over her chest. "I think I should go back to the hotel. It's only until next weekend, and then I move in down the street."

"Like hell. I won't let you go back there alone."

"I think I can handle myself."

"Shauna, that's not the point. This guy is raping and killing—"

"Young girls. I'm not a teenager."

Tossing the dishtowel aside, he stared at her. "Again, not the point."

"The point is: I can take care of myself."

"It's not safe. He knows too much."

"Stop being so damned noble. Just because we slept together doesn't give you the right to tell me what to do." She tried to move past him.

He blocked her path. "Sleeping together has nothing to do with it. I'm just being smart."

"I'm not your responsibility." Her eyes were full of venom.

"We are each other's responsibility, partner. Like it or not, we're stuck with each other." He moved to let her pass.

As the day progressed, so did the frustration. By the time Monday morning rolled around, the tension was so tight that if it were a rubber band, it would snap. Shauna had slept in the guest room, and it was painfully apparent neither one of them had slept very well by the light pace of their morning run.

On Monday, they had an early appearance in court. Then they had loads of paperwork at the office. It was well past seven by the time they left for home. Travis was famished and in the mood to cook.

"Do you like fish?" He broke the silence as he drove them toward Jimmy's shop.

"I love all seafood." She took a deep breath and turned toward him. "Except oysters and caviar."

Travis took the turn into the parking lot. After shutting the truck down, he hopped out and decided to try a new approach. Friendship. He liked Shauna, and he couldn't get fired for that.

"Hi, Mrs. Kawalski. You look lovely today." Travis greeted the shop owner's wife. He took her hand and kissed it.

"When are you gonna call me Iris?" She scrunched up her wrinkled face when she smiled back at him.

"Never. What's the catch of the day?"

"Got some perch Jimmy Jr. brought down from the lake this morning."

"I'll take some."

"Who's this?" Mrs. Kawalski winked, nodding in Shauna's direction.

Travis shook his head as he took some seasonings down from the shelves. "I'm sorry. Mrs. Kawalski, this is Shauna Morgan, my new partner."

Mrs. Kawalski took her hand and held it. "My, you are a tall thing, aren't you? And pretty. I hope this boy is behaving himself."

Travis smiled. "I always do."

"You'd better." She gave Travis the evil eye. "So, honey, you got a boyfriend?"

Shauna's eyes widened. "No, ma'am."

"Good. Travis doesn't have a girlfriend, and Lord knows he needs one."

"Mrs. Kawalski, she's my partner."

"Even better. Look at my Jimmy and me. We have worked together, side by side, for over forty years. We've raised three kids, have eight grandkids, and we're still *partners*. Best way to be."

"I'll take it under advisement." Travis handed her forty dollars.

"You forgot your change," Shauna said, placing her hand on his forearm as they headed toward his pickup.

"No, I didn't." He peeled her fingers off of him, helped her into the truck, and then started driving.

"Talk about amazing."

"Just doing my part to help out." The truck rolled to a stop in the driveway, then he helped her out. Jimmy and his wife had always been kind and decent and constantly let people take advantage of them.

"Why is it that others are amazing, but you can't be anything other than ordinary?"

"Because I am ordinary." He glanced at her as

they made their way up the stairs. Ordinary, she was not.

"You're handsome, sexy, and hot. I'm barely touching on your good looks. You're a gentleman. Kind, considerate, and generous doesn't do you justice. Intelligent, without being arrogant, and, oh my, you're blushing. I guess we can add humble, too." She giggled.

"You're making my life really difficult." He tossed his keys on the table and turned. "I'm not all those things. I have faults, too, ya know."

"Name one."

"I have impure thoughts about you." He stepped closer, fighting his conscience. "All the time, all day, even at work."

She held her hand up against his chest. "And you can cook. I want my dinner."

Her skin felt warm and soft when he held her hand in his and kissed her palm. He stared into her eyes, seeing them flicker with passion. "Can you make a salad?"

"I think so." She yanked her hand back.

He wanted to be glad she was pulling away, but he was angry instead.

All through dinner, it was apparent she would be sleeping in the guest room. It was for the best, he kept reminding himself.

"Your apartment has an alarm system, right?" he asked as he watched her finish the dishes.

"The main door has a deadbolt and a chain. I'll buy one of those motion sensors and install it myself."

"What about the back door?"

"Stop, okay?" She glared at him.

"I can't help it."

He glanced at his vibrating cell. "It's Scott." He flipped open the phone. "Brown here."

"There's been another murder," Scott said.

Travis glanced at Shauna. She seemed to understand the look because she went for her purse and shoes.

"We're on it." Travis took the information and flipped his phone shut. "Let's put an end to this." He grabbed his keys in a huff.

This made too many dead bodies in one week.

11

No sooner did Shauna finish looking at all the information from this last murder when another call came in. She felt like she was reliving the worst parts of her life.

Travis had been giving her evil looks all day, making her feel worse. A few times he mentioned they needed to talk, but they were never alone anymore, which in her mind was probably a good thing. If he knew who she was, giving him time to cool off could only be seen as a blessing.

During this last investigation, the faceless rapist would flash in front of her. Each time it happened, it sparked a memory, but she didn't know if they were real or not. She kept a small journal, noting everything she could. The next time she had the chance, she'd spill her guts to Travis, but only him. It was time to give up the charade.

Over the course of the last few hours, they'd met with an array of law enforcement, putting into place a game plan. When she was finally alone in the office, Shauna's body trembled from the inside out. She tapped her pen on her knee and looked down at her cluttered desk. All sorts of lab reports lay piled on top of each other, blending into one another. She leaned back in her chair.

"That looks like a mess," Jeff said, standing in the doorway, whistling that damn tune.

"Organized mess," she tried to tell herself.

"Cops got any leads?"

Leads? That was a joke. "They've picked up three guys, and one's a possible. He fits the profile and has no alibi. What's that?" She pointed to a file that had "Princess" written on it.

"I did some fishing and found some possible computer perverts who might fit the Princess profile."

When he moved closer to her, the hair on the back of her neck stood at attention. Her heart skipped a beat as he sat on the edge of her desk. "Interesting." She flipped through the file and then one name jumped out at her. Why the hell would her stepbrother be on this list? "What do you know about Craig Nagle?" She looked up at Jeff.

Something about his eyes made her push her chair back.

"He roughed up a few prostitutes a while back, and he had a whole bunch of kiddie porn when the cops picked him up." Jeff smiled at her, letting his eyes drop down below her face. "So, how do you like your job?"

"What's not to like?"

"How's Travis treating you?"

She tried to make herself get over whatever it was that made her squirm when Jeff was around. "We work well together."

"Jeff." She heard the smooth, protective tone in Travis's voice as he spoke.

"Jeff has some interesting computer pervs here." She waved the file, breathing a sigh of relief. "Look at this one." Shauna made her way to Travis's desk, opening the file for him.

"The cops are picking him up as we speak." Travis slammed his finger on Nagle's name.

"Really? What for?" Shauna heard the hitch in her own voice.

"It would appear he hacked into the medical examiner's database and tried to fiddle with the latest Princess Killer's lab results." Travis's eyes narrowed.

"Do we get to talk to him?" She bit down on her lip, holding back a strong surge of acid from the pit of her stomach.

"As soon as you're ready." Travis opened the desk drawer where he kept his keys.

"Let's go." She returned to her desk and grabbed her purse, hoping Jeff would just leave.

He did, but not before he sent her a lingering

gaze, humming that annoying song. She chose to ignore it; she had bigger problems at the moment.

Travis didn't bother opening the truck door for her this time. Nor did he give her a chance to get buckled in when he squealed the tires, ramming the truck forward into traffic. At least two cars honked their horns at them. Now wouldn't be a good time to bring up her identity.

Unable to stand the silence a second longer, she asked, "You don't believe this guy Nagle hacked into the system, do you?" Looking out the window, her stomach swished and sloshed when she read the sign, "Welcome to Saratoga Springs."

"He's not smart enough, but then again, you already knew that, didn't you?" He turned and glanced at her. His eyes were cold and his face hard as stone.

"He's my stepbrother," Shauna admitted. "But then you already knew that, didn't you?" she added sarcastically, feeling the anger in Travis's stare. She opened the door before the truck came to a complete stop and jumped out.

After all the formalities were completed and introductions made, she and Travis were led into a holding room.

"Shauna? What are you doing here?" Craig's eyes widened, and his body stiffened.

Shauna flashed her badge, squaring her shoulders. Her stepbrother hadn't ever hit her, but he could be downright nasty. She'd allowed him to make her feel like less than a whole person. No way would she let him do that today.

"Un-freaking believable." Craig fell back in his chair. "How the hell did you manage that one?"

"I went to school." She tossed her badge on the table. "This is my partner, Travis Brown."

"You know I couldn't have done what they said. I barely even know how to use my stupid computer." His voice cracked and shook with each word.

"You're a lot of things, Craig, but bright is not one of them. Who has access to your computer?" Shauna tried to swallow, but her throat was so dry, she failed. Everything had to end today. She'd had enough.

"My ex-girlfriend did, until she moved out last weekend."

Travis tilted his head. "Her name?"

"Janet Hawthorne," Craig said.

"You know her, too?" Travis muttered.

"Can't say I've have had the pleasure. Where is she now?" Shauna tried to ignore Travis. First flaw. He could be a royal pain in the ass when pissed off.

"I don't have a clue." Craig glanced up at her. "Your dad's been trying to find you."

Shauna closed her eyes. "Why?" she asked, but she didn't really care. To her father, she'd been nothing but a constant reminder of her mother, the woman he blamed for his pathetic excuse of a life.

"We both tried when my mom died."

Shauna opened her eyes. The bright light in the very white interrogation room stung her pupils. She didn't have a feeling one way or another in her body for her stepmother, and she didn't feel the slightest bit guilty. However, she never wished the woman dead. "I'm sorry."

"Yeah, right. Couldn't find your brother either." The contempt oozed from Craig's lips, but his shaking hands gave away his fear.

She held the power right now, and it felt good. "Roger's probably dead, too. Where does Janet work?"

"Last I knew, she worked at The Hen House. Don is real sick. He had a heart attack a few months ago. While in the hospital, they found he had cirrhosis of the liver. I think he's dying," Craig rambled.

There wasn't a shred of grief anywhere in the list of emotions Shauna had for her family. The only thing she felt for her father at this moment was pity.

"Who's Don? Roger?" Travis asked. His hands were on his hips, and he looked directly at Shauna, fire flaming from his eyes.

"Don's my father. Roger's my brother. Who else has access?" Shauna asked Craig. She didn't have the time to explain it all right now. Travis and his thoughts would have to wait.

"Anyone who's been in the house, I guess." Craig's eyes shifted from Shauna to Travis and then back again.

"Any enemies who would want to set you up?" Travis asked.

"I've made a few recently, but Janet has more. She used to turn tricks for a guy by the name of Gus Mortelli. Not only did she quit, she took off with some drug money. He's real ticked."

"He's also an informant." Travis cracked his knuckles. "Jeff's used him to get information."

"Are they gonna arrest me? I didn't hack into anything." Craig's left eye twitched while his hands trembled in his lap.

"All depends on what they find on your computer. We'll be in touch." Travis put his hand on Shauna's back and pushed her out the door. "You've got a lot of explaining to do."

They spent most of the night working with a designated task force of various police agencies putting together a list of possible suspects. They also put together a national announcement in hopes of keeping runaways from train stations, bus terminals, and airports.

She was barely awake when they pulled into Travis's parking lot. They never really spoke to one another, just around each other. They'd been able to piece together certain things for the task force, but she could see in his eyes that he wasn't too thrilled with not being able to put it all together for them.

She'd done the best she could, gave them everything she knew. He'd have to understand she couldn't risk being pulled off the case. Incessant buzzing bellowed in her ears. She reached for the alarm she didn't remember setting.

"Ouch." A familiar voice coughed.

"Travis?" She kept her eyes closed as she pressed her hand on his face. "I didn't have a nightmare." She sighed, sitting up, realizing she was almost completely clothed. *Thank God.*

He, on the other hand, was beautifully naked as he swung his legs to the side of the bed.

"You wanted to look at something in my files. You were asleep when I came out of the bathroom. Too damned tired to move you." He twisted his neck, cracking it.

"I hate when you do that. Do you mind?" She gawked at him when he stood.

"Too damn tired to care." He staggered to his closet. "We have a meeting at eight with...oh, I have no idea, but we have to be at the office in an hour." When he came out of his closet, he had on a pair of sweats. "I'm sorry. I wasn't thinking."

She was thinking. Not a good thing when all she could think about was his delicious body. "Oh, umm, well."

"Cat got your tongue?"

"You should have woken me." She leapt to her feet.

"I thought about it, but I needed to sleep." He rubbed his jaw. "We need to talk, alone."

"I need a shower," she said, trying to push past him to the door.

"We could talk in there. Kind of like killing two birds with one stone." He stood directly in front of the doorway, his arm blocking her path.

"I don't think that's wise."

"I haven't done a wise thing since I met you." His hand held her forearm, pulling her close. When his soft lips brushed against her cheek, her body ignited. "But go ahead. I'll make coffee, and we'll talk this out."

"Thanks." The muscles in her thighs felt like Jell-O as she made her way around the corner into the bathroom.

The next few hours were filled with meetings and press conferences. The only lead they had was her stepbrother. Not a very comforting thought. Shauna didn't think she could take much more.

But she would have to endure another murder.

At the latest crime scene at a local hotel, the killer left a little calling card. Just for her. Her world crumbled down in her lap.

"What the hell does this mean?" Scott held up the plastic bag with the note inside.

The musty lobby pierced her nostrils as she fought the tears struggling to break free.

"Is that from your journal?" Travis whispered in her ear.

She didn't acknowledge him. She didn't have to.

"What does it say?" she asked, not wanting to touch it.

"You remember me yet? I'm coming for you, Shauna. You can't hide from me. Not anymore," Scott read the note; his harsh words crippled her speech. "Can you explain this?" he barked.

"He's just trying to rattle us. We've both been on the news the last two days. He's taking what the media is reporting and using it." She heard Travis say the words, but she knew he didn't believe them.

He was lying for her.

"The last time he pointed to me. It's a game," Travis added.

"You two are off for a few days. I want you to take till Monday. Hopefully, the dust will settle by then," Scott said.

"You can't take—" Shauna started to say but closed her mouth when she felt Travis step on her foot.

"Monday, my office at eight." Scott turned and stormed off.

Travis shoved Shauna toward his truck.

"How dare you! Are you just going to let him take us off the case?" She glared at him after they had settled in the pickup and skidded into traffic.

"Use your brain."

"I am—oh." She paused. "He only did that to save face and give us the weekend to dig to our heart's content."

"You got it, sweetheart. I thought we could take everything up to Jake. He's got a bunch of ideas he wants to share with us anyway." He turned to look at her briefly. "And you and I have to have a serious conversation before that happens." His hands gripped the steering wheel.

---

*T*he drive to Lake George was an exercise in self-control for Travis. When Jake had called the other day with the information on Shauna and the time frame of her short disappearance, he knew Jane Doe had returned. He should have seen it earlier. Hell, he knew it earlier, he just didn't want to believe another woman he cared for would lie to him...betray him like that.

First, there was her uncanny ability to read so much into the killer's motives.

Not ability, but personal knowledge. Okay, maybe some ability. He had to give her some credit.

Then there was her drive to catch this particular rapist. All the research she had done in school. No one put that much time into something unless...they had a personal stake in it.

It didn't get more personal than rape.

The missing journals had really thrown him. He had no idea what to make of that. At first, he thought the killer was just messing with them, daring them.

Pushing *his* buttons. But it all made sense now. The Princess Killer knew she'd returned and was enjoying his own personal game.

Bastard.

Travis glanced at the speedometer. He was doing ninety, so he eased off the gas pedal. Damn emotions were clouding his judgment.

She'd admitted she'd been raped. But omitted by whom. He tried to be mad that she had lied. She'd done everything to hide behind her identity. But he directed his anger toward a murderous psycho. The whacko had killed his sister, and raped the woman he...*no, he didn't.*

He looked down at her. She'd rested her head in his lap and had fallen asleep. He ran his fingers across her chin and took a deep breath, forcing his eyes back to the road.

"Damn it," he whispered as he gripped the steering wheel. She had been feeding him pieces of information all along, and he had been putting them together. But she didn't trust him enough to just come out and tell him.

Fear gripped at his heart. He knew the killer was coming after her. He'd have to find a way to protect her. But first, he had to get her to tell him the truth. He wanted that from her. He needed that from her.

He ran his fingers through her hair, keeping his eyes on the Northway. Part of him wanted to shake her, he was so mad. The other part wanted to take her in his arms and hold her, make everything all right for her.

She had put her life on the line, and he knew in his heart it wasn't just to catch the killer, but to stop him.

He shook her shoulder gently. "Wake up, sweetheart."

She rubbed her eyes, sitting up. "Where are we?"

"My parents' place." He pulled her out of the truck and into his arms.

"I can walk," she mumbled, nuzzling her face into his neck.

"Sure you can." Travis fumbled with the door, careful not to drop her. He moved down the hallway to his room. Gently, he laid her down on his bed.

She took in a deep breath and let it out with a sigh. Her body stretched like a cat. "Travis?" Her eyes never opened, but her arms reached out for him.

He wanted to take her in his arms, but he couldn't. Not until she told him.

"I'm right here, sweetheart." He slipped off her shoes, trying not to pay too much attention to her ankles. He loved her ankles.

"Stay with me," she said, barely awake. Her eyelids fluttered.

"I'm not going anywhere." He kissed her temple, then lifted her shirt up over her head. Then carefully, he slid her slacks down her hips.

With tender care, he placed her folded clothes on

the desk. The bed squeaked when she shifted. Looking at her, half-naked in his bed, he struggled with his emotions. He didn't want to hurt her, but he was going to have to make her relive the worst nightmare of her life.

Tucking her under the covers, he kissed her soft, full lips. "Rest. You're going to need it." He closed the door behind him, and with a heavy heart, headed down the hall toward the kitchen where he heard the soft tap at the back door.

Travis let Jake in without saying a word.

"Are you okay?" Jake questioned.

Travis cocked his head, then sat down on the sofa, staring out into the darkness. "Depends on how you look at things."

"Are you in love with her?"

"That, my friend, is a loaded question. She's two different people." Travis took another sip of his soda, then looked at Jake. "She's Jane Doe."

Jake turned and seemed to chew on that piece of information. "I thought so."

"She hasn't come out and told me, but all the facts are there." Travis stood. He had so many questions, and now he wasn't sure he could ask them. "She did all this just to flush him out."

"Payback can be a nasty business." Jake ran his hand across his head. "I should know."

"When I wanted to track her down, it was to get information, catch this asshole, and ultimately protect her. Not put her on the front burner." He'd never felt so conflicted in his life. Even the pain of knowing that Gina chose to abort their child didn't hold a candle to the fear that Shauna was in real danger, and she'd put herself there on purpose.

"Jane Doe had been a nameless, faceless person. Now, she's someone you care about. Someone you want to protect on a different level. That changes the game. Changes it for the killer, too."

Travis turned, his heart pounding frantically against his chest. "What are you thinking?"

"I'm thinking that this guy's a cop."

"Jesus."

"Look, this guy knows too much. If he's not one of your own, then someone's helping him." Jake rubbed his neck.

"She's not even safe here." Travis turned and looked into the house. She wouldn't be safe until this bastard was dead or behind bars. He almost preferred the first option.

Jake stood next to Travis and placed a brotherly hand on his shoulder. "Might want to have someone patrol around your brother's place. One way of getting to you, which means he gets to her."

Travis stretched his arms in front of him, clasping his hands and cracking all his knuckles. "If I'm going to get this guy, I'm going to have to keep Shauna out in the open. I wonder how long he's known who she is."

"I'd guess since right before she showed up. I've gotta get going. Call me—day or night."

Travis nodded, following Jake to the front door. "The only people who knew she was coming would be people in my office."

"Get me a list. I'll do some digging."

Closing the door, Travis got a sick feeling in the pit of his gut. He could be working side by side with the man who killed his sister and damn near killed Shauna.

"Damn it to hell." He tossed the empty soda can in the recycle bin and slammed the garage door closed. Standing in his parents' kitchen, he stared across the family room and down the hall to where she slept. He was angry, sad, scared, frustrated, hurt, resentful, and in love. All because of one woman. One woman who he had been searching for and avoiding at the same time. But now he had to make a decision.

He had come to a crossroads, and for the first time in years, he didn't know which road to take.

12

Easing himself onto the chair in the corner of his childhood bedroom, Travis lifted his feet and gently rested them on the foot of the bed where Shauna slept. She shifted under the dark-blue comforter.

A slight breeze slipped through the crack of the open window, carrying a mixture of boyhood memories and the night he'd shared with her. He had to keep reminding himself she'd been through hell and came back to help him, to help Marie, and all the other victims. And she did it at great personal cost.

While his blood pumped unevenly through his body, he tried to set aside her mistrust and understand the young victim. He focused on the innocent girl who'd been brutally raped and beaten. His heart ached for her. No one deserved that.

But every time he thought about climbing in bed next

to her, to hold her in hopes of taking away any pain she might feel, he saw the agent. The strong, independent woman who matched his abilities, that woman should've come forward. Her decision to hide her identity baffled him, especially after he'd confided in her.

He shifted his head to the left, then to the right, but the tension in his neck gripped his muscles, not allowing him any relief. "Damn," he whispered. Why didn't she trust him? Especially after all they'd uncovered together. She, of all people, should know that every little detail counted. Even those things that seemed mundane, routine, or even obvious, could set them on the right path.

Yet she had lied to him.

Dropping his head back, he pulled up a blanket and tried to force his body to rest. He hadn't been dozing long when he heard her stir. A faint glow filtered through the sides of the curtains as the morning sun struggled to make itself seen.

"I hope you didn't sleep like that," Shauna said as she sat up, pulling the covers to her chin.

"Don't think I slept much." He shifted in his chair. "You want to shower before we start?" His voice sounded cold and bitter even to him.

Her eyes narrowed, and she pulled the covers tight in her fists.

"I'll give you some privacy." He shot her an icy stare as he walked from the room. What he needed was a stiff drink. He took a cold shower instead, then dressed without the usual routine. Everything right now seemed out of place. A decent breakfast might help him put things in perspective.

Amazed by the amount of time she was spending in the shower, Travis slammed her plate of pancakes on the table. "You going to take all day?" he shouted down the hall.

"Are you going to be an asshole all day?" She glared at him, then stormed into the kitchen.

"That all depends on you." He poured her a cup of coffee, gripping the pot handle to hide his trembling hands. He wasn't sure if he wanted to throttle her or hug her.

"I didn't do anything wrong." She took her coffee and blew into it, pushing the steam away from her face.

"Some people might not see it that way."

"Screw you and those people." Coffee splattered on the counter when she slammed her fist down. "Go ahead, ask me. I dare you."

"I'd like it if you told me instead."

She let out a dry chuckle. "Maybe I want to lie to you just a little while longer."

"Come on." He glared at her. "You owe me."

"Look, I was just a scared kid who didn't want to talk about it. I thought it was my fault, that I'd done something to deserve it. The cops were yelling at each other. All I wanted to do was get the hell out of there." Her fierce gaze collided with his.

"That doesn't explain why you're choosing not to tell me now. You still haven't told me." The disappointment in his tone was unmistakable.

"Back then, I didn't know how to defend myself. The only thing I knew, or believed, was that I was a no-good slut who would never amount to anything better than a call girl." She slammed her cup on the table. "It took a long time and a lot of counseling for me to learn how to live with what happened."

"That was then," he said softly, holding her angry gaze. "I want you to tell me now."

"Why tell you when you already think you know the truth?" She wiped the tears from her cheeks.

"Just say it, that's all I'm asking," he said behind a clenched jaw.

"Fine. You want to know who I am?" He could see her struggle for control, but he needed her to say it. "I'm Jane Doe. I was raped and beaten by an animal who is still out there, waiting for me to come back so he can kill me. You happy?"

"No." Holding his arms out to her, he took a step closer. Her hand landed dead center in his chest, stopping him, but it was the coldness in her eyes that made him physically back away.

"I spent years in counseling learning how to cope with what happened. It wasn't easy, but I'm damn proud of who and what I have become. I'm not going to let anyone take that from me."

"Shauna, I understand—"

"Like hell you understand." Her eyes looked as if they burned with vengeance. "All you see is what I was, not who I am."

"That's not true, and the only thing I don't understand is why in God's name you didn't tell me you were Jane Doe when you knew, even before you met me, how important she was…is to me."

A sarcastic laugh came from her mouth. "Jane Doe isn't important to you. I'm not important to you. The only thing you care about is catching the bastard."

"Yeah. I want to catch the asshole."

"But that's all you're focused on."

"And you're not?"

"It is something I want, but it's not what I live for. It's not just about finding my rapist. Marie's rapist. It's about helping to put an end to these types of crimes. It's about helping the victims. Not me, personally. And that is the difference."

"I do not live solely for this case."

"Yes, you do. I don't think you have a clue as to what you will do if and when you find this killer. You're so consumed with it that you can't see beyond it."

"Eat." He pushed the plate of pancakes in her face, unable to look her in the eye. She had a point, but he did care about other things. Namely her. But he'd have to deal with that issue later.

She pushed the plate away.

"Come on, Shauna, you need your strength."

"Fine," she muttered, and then plopped herself at the table.

He placed his hand on her shoulder.

"Don't touch me." She shrugged it off and shot him a warning glare.

Her fork scraped the plate as she toyed with her food, taking only a few bites. He fiddled with the dishes, mentally kicking himself for being such a jerk. She had been through so much in her life, given up so much. The least he could do was be nice.

"So? What are you waiting for?" She stood up, then took another cup of coffee, and without looking back, she opened the sliding glass doors and went out on the porch.

He followed her out onto the deck. The bright sun hit his eyes, forcing the world to blur. "I don't want to grill you. I just want to know what happened, what you remember." He tilted her chin and looked into her eyes.

"I was raped." She yanked her head back and then sat down. "And I don't have a clue who did it."

"I know this is hard for you." He didn't want to put her through this, but he knew it was necessary for both of them.

"Just ask your damn questions." She sipped her coffee.

For a brief moment, he didn't have any questions. He couldn't remember a single one. It floored him. He'd been trying to track Marie's killer through Jane Doe, and Jane Doe had just shown up. "I need a pen and paper." He moved back into the house, trying to collect his thoughts.

Shauna took a deep breath and let it out in a huff. She didn't want to admit it, but she felt relieved. Even though she'd woken up with a sour belly, and the pancakes hadn't really helped, she felt better. Telling the truth seemed to give her some relief from her guilt.

It wasn't that she couldn't talk about what happened, but that she couldn't give Travis the answers he so craved. The answers he lived for. She did worry about what he would do when they caught the Princess Killer. His life seemed so empty. Or maybe put on hold.

Hell, she was worried because that was her life, too. Sure, she was in this to help others, but ultimately, she was no different from Travis. Her drive came from the need to catch one killer.

Travis returned with *her* file, a pen, and paper, his face pale.

"Let's get on with it," she snapped.

"This is not going to be fun for me either. Whether you want to believe this or not, finding you was never about hurting you. I want to catch this bastard, and I need your help to do it. Ironic, when you think about it."

"And I need yours." She rolled her neck. The sooner she talked, the sooner it would be over.

Her hands trembled as she took her file from him. "You were pretty close on everything. I ran away because my dad was drunk all the time. He treated me poorly and told me I would never amount to anything. Said I was a no-good whore like my mother."

He took in a deep breath and muttered some curse. "The scar?" He touched her back.

"I didn't lie to you. But our killer put his cigarette out on my back. He did that to those who *saved* themselves for him. He said it made us uniquely his. My stepmother just added another feature." She put her coffee down as the muscles in her stomach tightened.

"I don't know what to say."

"There is nothing to say." A gurgle rolled around, and her stomach cramped. She tried to swallow but couldn't. "I can't change what happened. It wasn't my fault. I know that. I'm not ashamed of it, but I'm worried about my job. This job means everything to me."

"Don't worry about that." His tone indicating that, once again, she could trust him.

She resented that trust sometimes.

"Where did he pick you up?" he questioned.

"The Albany train station. He told me he could help me. I knew it was a line, so I got on the train. I didn't know he'd followed me." She watched him jot things down, knowing she was just another witness to him. Nothing more.

"Did he take you from the train?"

"I saw him in the food car. He'd been talking to some other girl—no, a woman. Telling her about how he was a director in New York. I was intrigued, but I still didn't believe him."

"Did you go with him willingly?"

Her feet hit the floor. "Oh, yeah. Just got in his car and let him have his way with me."

Travis lifted his brow.

"He cornered me by the doors right before the next stop. I thought he smelled funny. Now I know it was ether. The next thing I remember, I was in some room. It had to be somewhere south of Albany. Maybe near the first stop. I assume it was some nasty, old motel. It smelled all musty and gross."

"So he drugged you," Travis said as he flipped the page on his legal pad. "Do you remember what he was wearing?"

"I don't remember his clothes, but I think he wore a dark-brown or black wig. I thought maybe he was bald or something and didn't want anyone to know. Later, right before I jumped from the car, I could tell he had blond hair. He also wore a Yankees baseball cap."

"Physical description." He wrote so fast, she could barely focus on anything other than his hand movements.

"I don't remember."

"Don't think of yourself as his victim. Think like an agent. Think like you do when we're working." He squeezed her shoulder.

She knew Travis was right. She needed to compartmentalize. She needed to approach this like a trained professional. Be detached. Sitting up, taking the cool breeze into her lungs, she felt renewed strength.

She closed her eyes and let the memories come to her. "Grayish-blue eyes. Almost smoky. I don't think he was too big, and he wasn't heavy, but strong. He had a beard and a mustache, but for some reason I think the beard was fake. Every so often I see him with only the mustache. He wasn't ugly, but I don't recall him being all that attractive either." She opened her eyes. "Then again, I was only fourteen. 'Attractive' was the kid from *Growing Pains*."

Travis gave her a slight smile, making her feel at ease. "Okay, that could be any number of guys, but it's a start. Tell me what kind of things he said to you."

She swallowed, noticing that Travis did the same. This was not easy for either of them. His sister hadn't survived. "When I woke, he told me if I was still, it wouldn't hurt so much."

"Were you clothed at the time?"

The first tear fell. No matter how hard she tried to step outside herself, what happened was real. Her therapist told her there would be moments she'd feel completely and utterly stripped of her strength, but in order to get to the other side of those emotions, she had to play it out.

She had to tell Travis all of it.

Not only would it free her, maybe it would free him.

"This is hard for me, too. I keep thinking about Marie, and how terrified she must have been. I think about all those other girls. None of them deserved this. But I also think about you." His fingers warmed her skin as he brushed away her tears. "I'll admit that Jane Doe was another victim I wanted to talk to, but Shauna Morgan is real flesh and blood, someone I care about."

Pushing his hands away, she shivered. "I can't deal with that right now, okay?"

"All right," he said, sounding none too pleased. "Did he rape you there?"

She nodded.

Snap.

"Shit," Travis spat as blue ink dripped out of the

ballpoint pen that he'd snapped in half. "Sorry." He wrapped the pen in paper, turning from her.

"Your sister was found in a motel room. He might not have had the chance to set the stage, but the ones who he believed waited for him, he killed quickly. He didn't want to cause them any more pain than he had to. If I hadn't fought back, he might not have beaten me."

"That's sick." Travis stood, tossing the plastic end table over the railing. It bounced and rolled down the hill toward the lake, finally landing on the dock. "Damn it." He raked his hands through his hair. "I've talked to rape victims before. Some say they prayed for death." His voice shook with agony. She knew the pain was for his sister. Not her. She understood more than she wanted to.

Feeling the need to comfort him, she stood and took him by the shoulders. "I didn't want to die. I doubt Marie did either."

"What the hell is that supposed to mean?" He glared at her.

"Take your own advice." At this point, she didn't have the energy to hold his hand through this. "You had to know how hard this would be on you, to talk to me like this. It's as if you're hearing Marie tell you what happened."

"It's worse." Sitting back down, he grabbed the paper and a new pen. "How many times did he rape you?" he asked through gritted teeth.

"Once. He told me that because I had waited for him, he would make sure God took care of me. He made me get dressed, and that's when I tried to run. He beat me, blindfolded me, and put me in the car. He said he was going to end my life quickly. I shouldn't suffer, but I had to die. I didn't want to just then, so I jumped from the car."

The inside of her stomach swished and splashed like a pitcher of water falling off a table. "Oh, God." She moaned, running through the screen door. Gagging in her hand, her feet suddenly came off the floor, dangling in midair. Before she knew what was going on, she was on her knees in front of the toilet.

She rocked back on her heels as the second wave of nausea hit her. There was nothing left in her stomach, and a cold sweat broke on her forehead as she coughed until she was able to catch her breath, mortified he hadn't left.

No. He leaned against the sink, saying nice things to her, keeping her hair from falling in her face and rubbing her back. "You okay?"

"Just freaking great." She stood and gripped the sink, trying not to succumb to the nausea again. Turning the cold water on, she splashed it in her face and rinsed out her mouth. So much for trying to look halfway decent. "Let's get on with it." Without looking at him, she moved past him and grabbed all the other files, taking them out on the porch.

He must have stopped in the kitchen because he

came out with some crackers and soda. "This should help settle your stomach."

Wanting to stay focused, she said, "I don't think he was much older than twenty. His voice was distinct. I would recognize it if I heard it, but I doubt I would recognize his face. Every time I conjure it up, it's different." She joined Travis in making notes.

Hours flew by as they passed papers back and forth. She filled in all the blanks that she could, and he did the same for her.

"What's this?" She took a list of names.

"Suspects," he said dryly.

"Scott…as in…our boss?" She looked at him, stunned.

"He has a Yankees cap and grayish eyes, but I don't think he's our guy." Travis dumped his feet on the railing.

"Holy shit." She stared at the list. "These are all agents or cops."

"Going by something Jake suspected."

That really got her attention. "You think our guy is a cop." She'd never made that connection, but as she said it, it made perfect sense.

"I don't want to believe it, but stranger things have happened."

"I don't know most of these other guys." She held the paper in her trembling hands. "We're screwed."

"Are you sure about the voice?" He started gathering up all the papers.

She stood and looked over the lake. Was she sure? "I don't know." She bit back tears. "I've had conversations with at least five of these guys."

"It's okay to cry." His arm came around her.

She stiffened. Crying was out of the question. "Jeff's eyes are the right color."

"And Steve?"

"His eyes are cold and unnerving, but I'm not sure." A few salty drops fell, but she was determined to remain professional. She had to. "I thought I'd know when I heard his voice."

He took her by the hand and pulled her through the house, grabbing his keys.

"Where are we going?"

"You're not going to like it." He started the engine after they climbed into his pickup.

She didn't like it already. "Do I have to guess?"

"Home."

"Albany?"

"No." He gave her a pointed look.

Did he mean to take her home? As in Saratoga? Her father? "Nuh-uh. No way. I won't, you can't make me." But she knew it was necessary. "Crap. Don't leave me alone with my father."

Travis put his hand on her neck. "I won't let him hurt you anymore."

She laughed without any humor. "I'm not afraid of him, but he should be very afraid of me."

He pulled the truck into a gas station. Shutting the

engine off, he turned, cupping her head and pulling her face close to his. "You'll have to wait in line behind me." His lips brushed hers, then he got out and filled the tank.

She'd wanted to believe that encounter had been for her, but she knew, deep down, all his emotions were wrapped up with Marie. She'd filled in the blanks with what happened to his sister.

Forcing herself to forget his tender touch, Shauna focused on the papers they had created earlier. She didn't want to think about seeing her father. The last time she saw Don Morgan was the last time he'd hit her. She'd had to go to graduation with a black eye.

The closer they got to Saratoga, the more her body twitched. Setting aside the papers in their files, she turned to Travis. "I don't think I can do this."

His hand rested on her shoulder. "We need to find out who came and got those journals, and when."

"My dad's a drunk and won't remember squat, except that maybe I owe him money."

"You'd be surprised what a drunk can remember." They pulled into the driveway of an old, run-down shack.

Touching the butt of her gun, she took a deep breath and let it out in a puff. "I'm a trained professional." She stiffened her shoulders and took the lead. Travis's footsteps followed close behind her.

Looking around the overgrown lawn, she held back a sneeze from the white dandelions flapping in the breeze. She could almost smell the whiskey on her father's breath. Instinctively, she raised her hand to her cheek, the favorite landing spot for his fist.

Travis's fingers rested on her back and gave her the strength she needed to raise her hand to knock on the door. She prayed he was home. No way could she drive down that road again.

A lump caught in her throat the moment the door rattled. Travis's hand applied just enough pressure to remind her she was acting as an agent, not a victim.

The bald, disheveled man standing before them was not the man she remembered.

"May I help you?" Don Morgan asked.

She stared at him while he rubbed his unshaven jaw. His wrinkled face looked discolored, and there was a glazing over in his left eye. Looking down at him, he seemed smaller than she remembered. "Pop?" she questioned.

"Shauna?" His eyes went wide. "My, God. Is that really you?" He reached out, almost touching her, but pulled back as if he'd been burned. Then he just stood there and gawked at her.

"Sir, we need to ask you a few questions." Travis flashed his badge.

Shauna felt the nudge in her spine. Dropping her gaze to her purse, she pulled out her badge.

"A cop? My deadbeat daughter?" Her father stepped aside, waving them in.

"Actually, FBI, Pop." Shauna looked around at

what she used to call home. A layer of dirt and dust lined every inch of the old house. The stench of whiskey filled her nostrils. "Have you seen Craig lately?" She stopped at the doorway to the kitchen and blinked. This man got his kicks out of beating her. She shouldn't feel sorry for him.

But she did.

Being human really sucked.

"Not in a few weeks. He in trouble?" Her father offered them a shot.

Travis put his hand out, shaking his head. "We're investigating a case that may involve him," Travis said, glancing around. "When Shauna moved out, what did you do with everything she left behind?" Travis had both hands on his hips, giving her father a level stare.

"Roxie wanted to sell it, but I figured Shauna would be back, just like when she was a kid and ran away. You never came back." He downed a shot. "Just like a rat leaving a sinking ship."

"Answer his question, Pop."

"About two years later, your bigwig boyfriend came and picked everything up. Had official papers and everything."

"What was his name?" Travis said behind a clenched jaw.

"Why don't you ask her?"

"What did he say he did for a living?" Shauna asked.

"Just came here with papers and a really expensive suit. Said if I didn't give him all your stuff, he'd have to call the cops. Nothing of value. Just clothes and some old books. What does this have to do with me?"

"Nothing. Name, Pop. Give me a name."

Her father stared at the ceiling. "I don't remember." He sat down at the table, pouring another shot.

"What did he look like?" Shauna couldn't hide the agitation in her voice. They were getting closer.

"Like I said, expensive suit. Clean cut. Not the typical loser I would expect from you." He tossed another shot back.

"No worries, Pop. He wasn't my boyfriend." Shauna nodded toward the door. She had to get out of the house, but more importantly, she had to check on something. The killer had her stuff for the last eight years. This guy wouldn't just hold on to it. He'd try to bait her or leave Travis clues. Flaunting it in front of the cops always turned these guys on.

There was always the theory that psychos wanted to get caught, and maybe that was true in the end, but guys like her attacker liked to toy with the cops. He wanted to be able to say, "I was right under your nose. I left you every conceivable clue, and you still didn't know it was me. I had to tell you."

Travis tossed his card on the table. "Call if you can remember anything else."

She pulled him by the arm, rushing toward the

truck. Her stomach twisted and turned. "Not again." She moaned and dropped to her knees by a large tree in the front yard. Once again, he didn't have the decency to let her puke in private.

Wiping her mouth, she got back up to her feet. "Will you ever let me do that in peace?"

"What the hell did you eat yesterday?" Travis opened the door for her.

"Whatever you fed me."

"Yeah, well, I'm not sick." He handed her a mint.

"Just wait." She pulled out the files and started skimming the pictures.

"What are you doing?"

"Our friend took my stuff. I never thought about it before, but what if he left clues all along?"

"Damn. Hadn't thought about that."

She looked up to meet his warm eyes. He had a way of making her realize how much she had going for her. It was too bad that when this was over, she would be leaving the FBI behind. That meant leaving the best thing that had ever happened to her. The one man she could love.

And she did love him.

A fact she couldn't deny anymore.

A mixture of excitement and fear pumped through Travis's bloodstream as they pulled out all their files and laid them on his parents' kitchen table. They were getting closer. It was just a matter of time, but they had to unlock the mystery before the killer came after Shauna.

Shauna had tagged every picture with things that could have been hers. He was amazed she'd even noticed a pair of earrings her brother had given her for her tenth birthday. Travis gave up and watched her. When she worked, unfortunately for him, it was a major turn-on.

She glanced over the paper she held in her hands. "What?" It looked like she was holding back a smile.

"You're very special."

She shook her head. "I'm hell-bent on revenge."

"Justice." He corrected her.

She rolled her eyes. "Same as you, right?"

"Yep." Travis took some of her notes. "No way I could've done this." He tossed the paper at her.

"That's mostly personal knowledge. Not good work."

"It's both." He wanted to take her by the shoulders and shake her. Her talents in the field were being wasted. She was smarter than any other agent he had ever met. Her instincts were keener than a bloodhound's, and he wanted the chance to prove it. "Our next case, I'll prove it to you."

"There won't be a next case." She turned from him. "After this case is over, if I'm not fired, I'm going to ask to be transferred."

"Why?" He stood, pulling her with him.

Her eyes dug into him like an arrow. "You were right about me being obsessed with this case."

"I think we both have been slightly obsessed."

"To the point it's not healthy for us. I need to put this part of my life behind me."

"All of it?" He stared at her in disbelief.

"Yeah. All of it." She glared back.

Well, then. He took a deep breath. "What'll you do?" he asked with a sudden sharpness in his chest. Ducking his head into the refrigerator, he got himself a beer.

"There are a lot of violent crime units out there, and I can still do my work on victimology." She leaned up against the sliding glass door overlooking the lake. "But staying here will only be living in the past. It's time for me to move forward."

Travis guzzled his beer. This was it. She would walk out of his life forever. It should've made him happy. He had given up on finding a good woman, an equal to share his life with. That had all died when Gina aborted their baby.

Then Shauna had to walk into his life and complicate things. Big time. She stirred things in him. She made him want to be a better man.

She made him want to love again, but obviously she didn't feel the same way.

"Fine then. Let's catch this guy so you can have a life."

A life without him.

13

Travis stared at the steam seeping from the coffee machine as it filled the kitchen with gurgling noises. After pouring himself a cup, he stared into the hot, black liquid. He hadn't slept well. Thoughts of Shauna filled his mind and squeezed his heart. Stepping outside, the humid air almost suffocated him. With no breeze, the lake looked like glass. The stillness did nothing to help the emptiness he felt.

Damn her for making me feel again.

And the timing couldn't be more wrong. At the moment, all he wanted was to hop in his parents' sailboat and float about the calm lake, getting good and drunk. The last thing he wanted to do was spend the day going over files. He balanced his mug on the dash of his truck before he turned the key. Twelve years was too long to be tormented by one man.

Travis headed toward Jake's house. When Lana had first introduced Jake to Travis, he saw a hard military man who seemed to be a soldier lost without a cause. Later, Travis found out he hadn't been too far off the mark. War had changed Jake. He'd seen things that haunted his soul, until he'd met Lana.

Travis pulled into the driveway and waved to Katie.

"Gumby!" Katie greeted him in the doorway with Lana.

"Hi." Travis lifted her high in the air, then pulled her in for a big hug.

"Daddy's in his office. Where's your girlfriend?" Katie pinched his lips together, giving him a pouty kiss.

The smell of baby shampoo filled his nostrils. "She's still sleeping." He sighed, not bothering to correct the little girl.

"Let's go, sweetie." Lana took Katie from Travis. "You have about two hours before the twins wake up." She grabbed her purse and headed for the door.

Travis entered Jake's office only to find him standing with his back turned, rubbing his neck. That usually meant bad news.

"I don't like the look of this," Travis said.

Jake turned. "I did some digging on Ramsey and Wilcox."

Travis slumped himself into one of the brown leather chairs that faced Jake's desk. "Bring it on."

"Ramsey was brought up on sexual harassment charges in the Buffalo office."

"I thought it was an unfounded accusation." This wasn't news to Travis.

"Charges were filed, and then the woman who complained withdrew them and resigned from the bureau shortly after. In the beginning, her lawyer reported that they had at least two other agents willing to come forward." Jake sat down, resting his back against his chair and made eye contact with Travis. "He was transferred to your office. By request."

Travis clasped his hands behind his neck and stared at the ceiling. "That doesn't make him a rapist. He thinks women belong in the kitchen and makes no bones about it."

"What do you know about Wilcox?" Jake asked with a certain edge to his voice.

The question made Travis's stomach roll. "Very little. He's been at the Albany office forever. I think since he started. Hell, I think he grew up there."

Jake took out a file and handed it to Travis. "He's done more than grow up there."

Travis flipped through it. "Jesus," he muttered. Travis stared at an article about Jeff and his prom date, who had ended up missing and murdered. "This is fifteen years old." He lifted his gaze to stare at Jake. "Was he arrested?"

How the hell could he be an agent?

"He was never really a suspect. The victim's stepmother and dad said they watched him drop her off right after the prom. The father was the first suspect, and then two other boys at her school. They ended up arresting some kid who shot himself shortly after he was released on bail."

Travis stood and paced with the file still in his hands. "Shit." He pulled out the picture of the crime scene. It was in an old, run-down cabin on the Hudson. "She was found in her prom dress?"

"For whatever reason, this guy has been killing her over and over again." Jake handed him a piece of paper. "Wilcox was very cooperative with the cops. His story was airtight. I dug up some of his early records, and his psych eval states he's an overachiever, highly intelligent, but with some tendency toward grandiose behavior. The shrink who did the eval handwrote a note saying Wilcox was arrogant, but otherwise normal."

"I once heard a profiler say that some of the most notorious killers were some of the smartest creatures out there."

"My military record says I'm arrogant and not good at following orders."

"Doesn't make me feel any better." Travis leaned up against the doorjamb. How could he have been so blind? He had been working side by side with him for the last four years. "Shauna thought for sure she would recognize his voice."

"She was a teenager and frightened for her life. Her memory's clouded. Wilcox was in the drama club in high school and had an uncanny ability to do impressions. Are you gonna tell Shauna?"

Travis craned his neck to the left, then the right. "I don't know. One minute she's focused, then the next moment, she's puking her guts out. I can't tell if she's falling apart on me, or if she's just sick. I'm a bit worried about her coming face-to-face with him at the office." Even as the words left his mouth, he knew he'd have to tell her. Worse, they'd have to put her out there as bait.

"You have to arm her with this information." Jake gave him a piercing look.

"What if she falls apart?"

"Stop looking at her as the woman you care about, but rather as the field agent who is better than you."

"But this puking thing."

"It was probably something she ate. I'm sure she'll go after this guy with both barrels loaded."

"That could be a problem, too."

Moments later, he walked into his family home to find Shauna sitting down at his parents' computer, gripping the mouse so tightly that he thought it might crumble. Hoping not to scare her, he cleared his throat right before he touched his hand to her shoulder.

She jumped, taking a swing at him and connecting right in his gut.

"Humph."

"Jesus, Travis. Don't sneak up on me like that. If I had my weapon, I would have shot you."

Holding on to his aching gut, he coughed. "You should always have your gun." Trying not to wince, he forced his body upright. "Damn, nice hit."

"Nice abs. I think you bruised my hand."

"What's got you spooked?"

She tried to get to the computer before him, but he swatted her hand away. An old newspaper clipping of Jeff appeared on the screen. "Just wonderful." He cursed under his breath.

"You knew?"

"Just found out. Jake did some digging for me. Found a whole bunch of shit." In need of a drink, he led her into the kitchen. Instead of quenching his thirst, he leaned up against the counter and quenched his desire to touch her. "You okay?"

"Oh, yeah. Peachy." Her body trembled as she took a step back from him. "I've been working with the man who raped me and didn't even know it."

"Come on, Shauna. You were just a kid, and we don't know for sure."

"What about the voice? God, that voice haunts me in my dreams all the time—oh shit."

"What?"

"'Day Dream Believer' by The Monkeys."

"Have you lost your marbles?" Travis stared at her.

"That song. I remember it."

"It's a horrible song."

She shook her head. "You don't get it. The killer, he sang that song all the time. It drove me nuts because he actually sounded just like The Monkeys." She blinked. "Jeff hums that song. Damn it. I should've known." Her pupils widened. "And we do know for sure—Jeff's the Princess Killer."

"Jake did find out Jeff can disguise his voice, do impressions," Travis said.

"That makes me feel worse. I thought I'd hear him or something. But instead more girls died because of me."

"Stop that," he barked. "You're no more responsible than I am."

Letting out an exasperated breath, she leaned her hip against the counter. "Intellectually, I know that. But this whole thing just fucking sucks."

He knew exactly how she felt. His inability to put it all together, to make people see the things he saw, made him feel responsible for every girl who had died on his watch. "How's the stomach?"

"It's better, but I have so much nervous energy I can't stand it."

He could feel it, but who could blame her? "Will

you be able to face him at the office?" The look on her face told him she was more capable of facing that bastard than he was.

"I might castrate him, but not until he's in handcuffs."

He let out a chuckle. "You'll have to wait in line."

An awkward silence filled the kitchen. A soft breeze from the lake ruffled the kitchen curtains, bringing in the fresh scent of spring.

"I have to do this on my own." She folded her arms across her chest.

"We do nothing alone." He cocked his brow. "We're partners, and we watch each other's backs."

"I understand that, but you can't protect me from my past. I have to face it."

"I sure as heck can protect you from that bastard."

The breezed kicked up and swished her hair. "I don't want your protection, I want your help."

"One and the same."

"Please don't treat me like some little girl who needs to be protected from the big, bad wolf. I have a job to do, and I plan on doing it."

"And you'll do it with my help." The strength of her convictions and her sheer determination were something he could match. She'd get protection, whether she liked it or not. "When this is all over, we have a lot to talk about." He tucked a few stray strands of her hair behind her ear.

"I don't think so."

"Whether or not you stay here has nothing to do with us."

"You don't understand. I have to put this part of my life behind me. Close the door on it. On you. And you need to do the same."

"What the hell are you talking about?"

She didn't have time to answer because her words were cut short by the yelling coming from the dock. Yelling directed at him. Travis opened the door for his brother and sister-in-law who were yelling at each other and at Travis at the same time.

"Quiet down. What's the problem?" Travis closed the door, staring down at the boat. All three kids were huddled in the bow, wearing solemn looks. "You're upsetting your own kids."

"No, you're upsetting this whole family." Kim glared at him. "How dare you!" She poked him in the arm.

"What the heck did I do?" Travis studied her face. He'd seen that look the day he took Adam shooting at the range. This was a woman on a mission to wring his neck.

"I can live with Jake showing up all the time, hell, he's family. I can even handle a cop car going up and down the street. They do that all summer long anyway. But to have an unmarked car parked down the road, my dear brother-in-law, is over the top." She planted her hands on her hips.

Travis caught Shauna's eyes across the room as she

reached for her weapon and his keys. "Not without me, sweetheart." With a tender nudge, he pushed Kim aside. "Get the kids in this house, lock the doors. I'll call Jake and have him come down until we get back. Don't leave this house, understand?" He gave Bill his best cop look.

"You didn't put that car there?" Bill opened the door and motioned to the kids.

"Nope. You didn't happen to get a plate number?"

"I'm a biology teacher for crying out loud," Bill snapped.

"It was a dark, four-door sedan, I think a GMC, and there was one guy in the front seat," Kim added.

"What did he look like?" Shauna stopped short of the door.

"I didn't get a good look. Too pissed off," Bill said.

"All I noticed was a baseball cap."

"Yankees?" Travis asked.

"Could've been," Kim said.

Travis opened the door, jumped into the truck, and peeled out of the driveway. "Check out every car you see."

"No kidding, Sherlock," Shauna said.

By the time they pulled into his brother's driveway, there wasn't a dark sedan in sight.

Shauna leapt from the truck. "Come on, you bastard. Here I am! Come and get me." She stood in the middle of the driveway, waving her arms and moving in a circle.

"What the hell are you doing? Get in the car," Travis yelled.

The fire in her eyes frightened him as she slammed the truck door closed. "This has to end right now. I'm sorry I brought you into this mess."

"Brought me in? Are you nuts? I was knee-deep in this before you ever showed up." He rested his hand on her thigh. He had to touch her. Somehow he was going to make her see that leaving wasn't the answer. Running from him wasn't the answer.

"Because of me, he's…"

Her words hit Travis in the gut harder than her punch. "He's going to go after Jessica, use her to get to you."

She looked out the window. "I'll stay here and protect her."

"It can't be you. He'll kill you both without thinking twice. I'm not willing to risk it." He pulled her close to him.

"I won't be able to live with myself if anything happens to her because of me." She tucked her tear-streaked face into his neck.

"Come on, Shauna. We're going to nail Jeff." He kissed her forehead, running his fingers in her hair. He felt moist heat glide across his neck.

Then her lips came crashing down on his. She was wildly out of control. Her mouth demanded his participation. Before he had a chance to fully understand what she was doing, she was in his lap and pulling at his clothes.

For a brief moment, he went with it. Stroking the inside of her mouth, matching her passion with his own. She wanted to be loved. He felt the urgency in her touch, but this wasn't the right way, not now.

"Sweetheart." He separated their intertwined mouths. "Not the time or place." His thumb brushed away the tears.

"Oh, God." She bumped her head on the rearview mirror as she climbed off his lap. "I'm sorry. I just wanted to...to..."

"I understand." He put the truck in gear and started to drive back to his parents' house. They needed to meet with Jake and formulate a plan.

"He's not going to rape and kill you," she shot back.

"He might try to kill me, but if he lays a hand on you or my niece, he won't live to see my funeral."

Travis was done playing games. At this point, they could fire him, and he wouldn't care. He was going to nail this asshole and then get his life back. He hadn't realized how much power he had given to this man until Shauna had walked into his life.

Well, not anymore.

*S*hauna closed her eyes as the darkness crept in, bringing on night. The rest of the day had been spent trying to devise a plan that didn't include using her as bait. But she was the only bait they would ever have, and the only source that would make Jeff reveal himself. She had to put herself out there. Not something that Travis was too keen on.

She wasn't too keen on the idea either, but Wilcox would go after Jessica. History would repeat itself if she didn't stop him.

The drive back to Albany was about as tense as tense could be. Neither one of them could open their mouths without starting a fight.

Emotionally, she was spent. She felt like she could sleep for a week. Heading straight for the bathroom, she filled the tub. Breathing in the scent of her vanilla candles mixed with the bubble bath, she let her body relax.

Somewhere between sleep and awareness, she heard her name. Forcing her eyes to open, a blurred Travis came into sight. Startled, she splashed water about the tub, making the bubbles reveal a little more than she would have liked.

At least he had the decency to turn his back to her and hand her a towel.

"Sorry. You didn't answer when I knocked." He looked over his shoulder just as she wrapped herself in the towel.

"As you can see, I'm just fine."

"That you are. I wanted to talk to you."

The steam that had filled the room, along with her candles and his scent, made her insides go to mush. The worst of it was that she felt completely comfortable with him, and she didn't want to. There was too much pain attached to being with him. Every time he looked at her, he would see Jane Doe or his sister. Not Shauna Morgan. "Mind if I get some clothes on first?"

"I like you like this." His eyes roamed the length of her body. "You're a very beautiful woman."

She couldn't speak. She just stared at his wonderful smile, wanting to throw her arms around him. She almost forgot who she was. She let the air in her lungs fly out in a huff.

"Why are you pushing me away?" The soft caress of his thumb across her cheek made her muscles relax. But she couldn't give in.

"Every time you look at me, you'll see Jane Doe. And I'll see Marie's brother. It's a lose-lose situation."

His mouth opened, but she covered it with her hand.

"We got caught up in a whirlwind. I don't regret making love with you. I never will, but if you knew who I was, you would've never even considered it." She pulled her hand from his mouth.

"Maybe not at that moment, but I've considered you ever since I laid eyes on you." The tenderness of his eyes soothed her soul. Looking into them was a mistake.

While he had the comfort of a loving family, she kept the world at a distance. But both lived with the isolation of not wanting to find love. It hurt too damn much. And she had just proved it.

"You feel something for me. You can't deny it," he said behind gritted teeth.

"You'll see that there is nothing here when this is over." She tried to guide him to the door, but he smiled at her instead.

"I have an idea." His smile got wicked.

"That can't be good." She adjusted her towel.

"Give me one date after we put Jeff where he belongs." The smug, arrogant look on his face was too darn sexy.

"We can't date. There are rules about fraternizing."

"That's okay, because I'm going to work for Jake. I like the idea of being a P.I."

"Out!" She stomped her foot and pointed.

"It's a date." He turned and left, not closing the door.

She slammed it shut. "I want flowers!" she yelled. "And chocolate, and you better cook for me, or I won't go!" She stared at herself in the foggy mirror, wiping it with her hands.

She came out of the bathroom wearing sweats and an oversized T-shirt, with her hair in a ponytail.

No way would he find her attractive like this. "By the way, what did you want to talk to me about?"

His eyes scanned her body.

Okay, maybe he was an odd duck.

"Oh, we have a few days to dig. Jeff got called to Syracuse." Travis's face hardened immediately.

She rubbed her arms. "Can we get into his apartment?"

"Not 'we.' *Me*."

"Like hell, *partner*." She tilted her head, daring him to take her on.

He stood inches from her, hands on his hips with a mean scowl. "I won't have you breaking the law."

"Save the nobility. It's my ass on the line. Not yours." She spread her stance, locking her hands behind her back, not willing to back down.

"I take personal pride in that adorable ass of yours. I plan on grabbing it while on our date."

She refused to crack a smile. He would have to crack first.

He copied her cop-like stance, with a stone-cold face. Just when she thought her knees would buckle, he laughed. "Good Lord. I have met my match and then some." He shook his head. "How are you feeling?"

She held her stomach. "I'm fine." She wondered if she had eaten something that was bad. It wasn't just the shock of the last few weeks and seeing her father. Her stomach had been off for a while. "Actually, I was hoping for a bagel or something."

He squeezed her shoulder. "I ran to the market and got some mini bagels." He walked to the kitchen, pulled out a bag, and tossed it to her. "Butter?"

She made a face as her stomach flipped over again. "Plain is good." She sat down at the table as he poured two glasses of water.

"We can't prove that he raped you or my sister." Travis straddled the chair.

She broke off a piece of her bagel. "Do you think we can leave my identity out of it?" She popped a small piece of the bagel into her mouth.

"That depends on him and how we go about telling Scott."

She closed her eyes.

"You're not coming with me," he said with a clipped tone.

She swallowed hard. "You don't have a choice. I'll follow you or sneak out on my own. But, as you so bluntly pointed out earlier, we're in this together, whether you like it or not."

"I like being together with you in general, but—"

She shoved a bagel in his mouth. "No buts. I'm going with you so stop trying to save me."

He threw his hands in the air. "I'm not being noble, just sensible."

"If you were being sensible, you would stop arguing with me and drop the male ego thing."

The corner of his mouth went up. "You give me too much credit. If I was hung up on the male ego thing, I would seduce you just because I can."

Her mouth opened, sucking in a breath, and making a horrible gasping noise. "Not."

"Shall I prove it?" His lips were so close to hers, she already tasted him. "Close your eyes," he whispered.

She heard his chuckle when she complied right before his lips brushed hers.

She didn't mean to moan, but his mouth was soft and warm. The moment her lips went cold, she opened her eyes.

His blue eyes were hazy with lust. She would make love with him, if he asked. "Kissing doesn't constitute seducing."

"You're right." He scowled, standing up. "I'm tired. I'm going to run in the morning."

"Works for me." She grabbed a couple of bagels and headed to her room, confused. He went from red-hot to ice-cold in seconds, and something she did or said made him that way. She should be glad he went cold. But she was lonely instead.

A taste of love was enough to make her never want to feel it again, except with him. He made her want to go after some of her childhood dreams. He made her want to be herself.

Thoughts that haunted her sleep.

*T*wo days later, she found herself in a ridiculous black cat suit that even Nicole Kidman would look fat in.

Something crackled in her ear.

"Shhh, the whole neighborhood can hear you," she whispered.

"Then turn your volume down," came Travis's throaty response.

Well, that was stupid. She pulled out her binoculars and looked out of her bush in the back of the apartment building. Jake was parked in a truck on the street.

"Maybe the three of us should go into business," Jake said.

"You're kidding, right?" Travis commented.

"Hey. Watch it. I'd make a damn good P.I." Her, a private investigator? No. "Walkers," she whispered as a couple walked down the path behind the apartment complex. She looked up, seeing a flash of light fade. "Keep it low."

"I'm as low as I can get without belly crawling," Travis said with an agitated tone.

"Never mind the threesome. You two fight too much," Jake said.

Shauna rolled her eyes. If he wanted to see a fight, she could give him a real fight. She pictured Travis flat on his stomach with his hands behind his back and her holding them there.

Knock it off!

She had to get these crazy ideas out of her head. He constantly reminded her of their little so-called date. Which was never going to happen, because as soon as it did, he would have a light bulb moment, and loneliness would eat her alive.

"If you're planning on coming out, don't. Couple entering the building through the back," Shauna whispered.

"All clear here," Jake said.

Silence.

Shauna looked up to Jeff's apartment. "Travis?"

More silence.

"I'm going in." She took one last look around.

"You go up there, and I'll—"

She closed her eyes. "Next time, answer me. Are you coming down?"

"Already in the truck."

She took a deep breath, letting it out with a big whoosh. Jake rolled the truck to a slow speed in front of her bush. She jumped out and leapt into the open side door, pushing Travis's hand aside. "Jerk."

"Were you worried about me?" The truck jerked forward, and Shauna fell into Travis's lap with a thud.

She shook her head, thinking she should get off his lap. But damn it, she liked it. "What did you find?"

"It's clean." He squeezed her knee. "I suspected it would be."

So did she.

"It's sparsely decorated. Like he doesn't spend a lot of time there. Not much in the refrigerator."

"Kind of like leaving behind stuff at my place." He didn't live there.

Jake pulled into Travis's driveway. "I've got to get home. If I hurry, I might be able to catch my wife before she falls asleep." Jake didn't bother to get out.

"Thanks, man." Travis shook his hand.

"Don't mention it." Jake waved and drove off.

She closed her eyes in disgust when Travis looked her up and down as they climbed the stairs to his apartment. "I swear you got me this suit just so you could make fun of me."

"Sweetheart, I don't want to make fun of you." He closed the door and pinned her between him and the wall. "I want to make love with you."

Her chest tightened as the adrenaline kicked from his body to hers. "Life-threatening situations heighten sexuality," she huffed out in between short breaths.

"Heightens a lot of things. But that wasn't life-threatening." He pried open her legs with his knee and pushed slightly.

"Our bodies perceive it as life-threatening, so there is a rush of adrenaline." Her chest pressed against his, and she could feel his heart beating against hers. "You're not thinking straight," she said, dropping her gaze to his lips. At that moment, she knew she was a goner. Her lips trembled when she licked them.

"My only thoughts are how to get you out of this suit and into my arms."

The wetness of his tongue teasing her lips sent a warm tingle down her spine. "I'm already in your arms." She closed her eyes, feeling him against her. It didn't matter that he only wanted her because he had been in an extreme situation and his body was reacting to the possible danger.

She wanted to be filled by him. One last time.

"But you're still in this." He tugged at the tight fabric against her waist.

She knew nothing would ever come close to this feeling again. "I had to wiggle to get in it."

His head dropped against the wall next to hers.

"You okay?" She tugged at his hair.

He leaned against her. "Can I watch you wiggle out of it?"

His hardness pushed against her intimately, making her go dizzy. She pulled his head from the door, searching his passion-filled gaze for one good reason she shouldn't kiss him. Finding a million reasons she should push him away, she ignored every single one. Cupping his face, her mouth devoured his.

Without any grace, she pushed him from the door and took him down on the floor. Straddling him, she felt the cold air on her back as he pulled the zipper down from her spandex suit. While she bruised his lips, he tried to pull the suit down over her shoulders.

Prying her mouth from his, she sat up and tried to help.

"Wiggle." He tugged. "Oh, God. So glad I didn't know that." He stopped and stared at her bare breasts.

"Bra lines are just as bad as panty lines," she said.

His grip tightened on her behind.

Being empowered had never been so appealing to her before. She never wanted to use her sexuality in any way, but right now she enjoyed toying with him. More than any woman had the right to.

"Anything?" His eyes were wide, and his hands were wild with pressure.

She smiled and shook her head. Next thing she knew, she was on her back, and he was trying to get the suit over her hips.

"Wiggle."

She knew he was trying to be playful, but his voice was smoky and hot. "Not until you take off your shirt."

He ripped it off in one swift motion. "Now wiggle." He tugged.

She complied.

His lips touched her stomach as he managed to remove the tight article of clothing. "I love your body," he said between kisses, moving up her body to her breasts. "Everything about you is perfect." He took her nipple into his mouth.

She arched her back, reaching for his belt buckle,

not knowing he had already undone it. She finished with his button and zipper, releasing his firm shaft in her hands. "Now." She guided him to her.

He didn't hesitate, pushing himself inside her with a deep groan.

Sliding her hands in his pants to grip his half-exposed rear end, she encouraged him to pick up the pace. She rocked her body, searching for that release only he could deliver. Her body didn't let her down. With one leg wrapped firmly around his butt and the other tucked up under his arm, her body convulsed in an even more powerful orgasm.

One that seemed to go on forever.

Holding him tight, she tried to catch some air. It took some work, but shortly, they both started to breathe normally again.

"I love these legs." He rose up on one elbow and rubbed her thigh.

"You love what I can do with them."

"I didn't even carry you to the bedroom." He kissed her nose.

"We wouldn't have made it," she teased. This was more fun than she had ever expected. "I was right about you."

"Huh?" He jerked his head back.

"About the kind of lover you'd be."

"You said kind and considerate. I didn't consider anything but getting inside you."

"I tossed you on the floor. You just gave me what I

wanted." Oh, boy, did she want him right then and there.

He closed his eyes and shook his head. "If you want to believe that, go ahead."

"If I had just followed your lead?"

"Bedroom," he admitted.

"If I had asked? Or questioned."

He frowned. "Okay, you win. I would have given you whatever you asked." He started to get up.

She squeezed her legs around him. "Whatever I ask?" She stroked his buns.

"Can I have a five-minute break?"

"Long enough to make it to the bedroom." She giggled, feeling him kick off his shoes. He stood, helping her up and hiking up his pants at the same time.

She kissed his neck as he carried her into his bedroom. "You're something else."

He pulled back the covers and put her down.

"You really are one-of-a-kind, you know that?" She looked deep into his loving eyes.

He slipped out of his clothes, then turned the light off, leaving the small reading lamp on, and climbed in next to her. "Your knowledge of men hasn't been extensive, and those you did know were jerks."

He had her there, but she knew he was special. "Do you know any men like you?"

He rubbed his jaw as if he were deep in thought.

"Just say 'thank you' and accept the compliment."

"Thank you." He kissed her, wetly and passionately.

His five-minute break must have been up. Later, when she began to fall asleep in his arms, she wondered if she would ever get through a day without remembering what it felt like to be with him, to smell him, to love him.

She stifled her tears. Loving him felt right. When she was with him, she felt safe and free to be herself. To be Shauna.

How ironic was that?

14

Travis felt the warmth of Shauna wrapped around his body. The soft scent of fresh lilacs filled the room. "Good morning," he whispered as he opened his eyes. She lay on her back, snuggled up against him, and stared at the ceiling. Her face paled. "Oh, God. I'm sorry. I'll take them down."

She blinked, covering her mouth. "Please don't move."

"What's wrong?" He stilled when the blood completely drained from her face. "You feel okay?"

Taking in a few deep breaths, she didn't answer him.

"Jesus, I'm so sorry." He looked between her and the picture of her just hours after she'd been raped. That was enough to make him ill, but then he remembered: *Jeff.* She would have to face him sometime today. "You can call in sick." He ran his finger up and down the soft skin on her arm.

"I don't think so." She dipped her head toward him as she swallowed. "I have a job to do, and he's not going to stop me from doing it."

"All right," he said. "Have you always been like this? Getting sick when you're upset?" He kissed her shoulder.

"No. I must be coming down with something."

"I think you need to stay here." He moved gently from the bed, handing her his shirt and boxers.

"I think we both need to go to work."

The white T-shirt looked about the same color as her pale body. She pulled the shirt over her head with great care, then stepped into his checkered boxers.

"You sure?"

Covering her mouth, she walked to the bathroom with her head held high, then closed the door.

"Damn." The bed squeaked when he stepped on it and then tore the pictures down. How could he be so insensitive? She had to wake to seeing herself just hours after the worst day of her life.

When the water had shut off in the bathroom a few moments later, he threw on his running clothes and hurried toward the kitchen.

She had beaten him there, already dressed, and doing some stretches. Looking over her shoulder, she gave him a slight smile, her cheeks still pale.

"Are you sure you're up to this?"

She shot him a warning glare. "I didn't come back here just to run off when things got dangerous."

He nodded.

All morning, she remained silent, and he didn't press her. Seeing Jeff was going to be a test to both of them. He knew her well enough to know she might snap.

He might snap.

With every knock on their office door, she almost jumped out of her skin. Jeff was due back around four, and Travis needed to find a way to get her acting like her carefree self in the next hour. So he shot a small rubber ball at her that he had in his drawer from when Kamy had come to visit. Unfortunately for him, it landed right on her breast. "Sorry." He tried not to smile.

"Yeah, right." She tilted her head, looking down the hall, and rubbed her breast. "Oh, sorry." She rubbed it one more time for his benefit, smirking at him.

"Yeah, right." He laughed.

She smiled, relaxing back in her chair, just in time.

Jeff stood in the doorway. "If I didn't know better, I'd say there's definitely something going on with you two," Jeff said, then waltzed into the office.

Travis tore his gaze from Shauna, and his body went rigid with rage. He stabbed a pencil under his desk against the wood; it cracked. "Get a life."

"Craig Nagel was arrested this morning." Jeff looked directly at Shauna.

Travis tried not to ball his fists. Keeping his cool under these circumstances was something he'd spent the better part of his life learning how to do. Today would be a testament to that training. "What for?"

"Beat the crap out of his girlfriend. Guess what they found in his apartment?" Jeff smirked.

Shauna moved across the room and touched Jeff's back. *Why the hell did she do that?*

The room spun around Travis. He had to focus to keep himself from seeing spots and reaching across his desk to grab Jeff's neck, putting an end to his life.

"Have anything to do with the Princess Killer?" Shauna stood close to Jeff. Too close.

"Smart girl," Jeff said with an eerie tone. "He had a box full of crowns."

Travis twisted his neck, cracking it loudly, wishing it was Jeff's neck. "I told you." Travis pointed his finger at Shauna, hoping to set the trap. Jeff had to think he and Shauna were on different pages. Amazingly, she seemed to be holding it together better than he was. "I knew he was up to no good."

"I don't think he's smart enough," Shauna said.

"I wouldn't be surprised if they booked him soon." Jeff squeezed Shauna's arm. She actually smiled at him, but her complexion faded.

Just enough that Travis knew he had to get one of them out of the office. "One more case wrapped up."

Travis took a file off his desk, he had no idea what it was, but he handed it to Shauna and then glanced at his watch. "They have enough to hold him for the night?"

"Unless someone posts bail for the beating, I think he'll be there for a day or two. Longer if they charge him with multiple rapes and murders."

"Thanks, Jeff," Travis sat back down, hoping Jeff got the hint.

"My pleasure." Jeff turned and walked out of their office with a horrid smile plastered on his face, humming that damn tune.

"Damn it," Travis said. His gut told him Jeff knew they were on to him. Travis heard the change in Jeff's voice, and Shauna looked like she might lose it right there.

"Excuse me." She walked past him, holding her stomach.

Travis stood in the doorway of their office as she barreled into the ladies' room. Jeff wouldn't do anything here. That would be a death wish. Then again, psychos usually hang themselves at some point.

Keeping a close watch on the hallway, Travis flipped open his cell phone and called his brother.

"Hello?"

"Jessica?" he questioned.

"That would be me."

"Put your dad on the phone," Travis said. "It's important."

"Nice to talk to you too, Uncle Travis," Jessica said sarcastically.

When Shauna made her way back into the hallway, it appeared the color had come back into her cheeks. But just as she took a few steps toward him, Steve managed to back her into a corner.

Once again, her face turned two shades of white.

"What's up?" Bill's voice echoed in Travis's ear.

"Stay close by. Things are about to turn ugly. I'm going to call Jake." He closed his phone, eyeing the scene in the hallway.

Shauna nodded and then made it back down to where Travis was standing.

"What was that all about?" Travis whispered.

"Not here." She eyed him with caution. "Let's go." She grabbed her purse, not giving him room to protest.

Pulling his keys from his pocket, he followed her, deep in thought. What did Steve say to get her to go white again?

---

*S*hauna didn't understand why her body was revolting so violently. She dodged Travis's questions, talking him into stopping at Jimmy's store to pick up dinner. She even talked him into going to her new apartment, saying it needed to look like she was living there. Thus far, she had only moved her car and some clothes.

Travis managed to find her a bed, a couch, and a television set, but that was about it.

Travis had settled on a chicken and rice dish that he thought might help calm her stomach. He rolled up his sleeves and started cooking. It amazed her how much she enjoyed watching him handle food.

Looking around the empty apartment, she decided with a little decoration, this place could be pretty cool. It was set up very similar to Travis's, but it had only one bedroom, and the kitchen didn't have room for a table. It had two barstools on the other side, almost in the family room, the only other room in the apartment.

"I wonder if I could paint the walls." She placed her elbows on the countertop, dropping her cheeks in her palms.

He glanced up while he chopped the sizzling chicken he'd just taken from the pan. "I don't see why not. How long is your lease?"

"I didn't sign a lease. We agreed to first and last month's rent. Then I have to give one month's notice."

Travis gave her a puzzled look.

"I told him if I stayed more than two months I would sign a one-year lease. Less, he could keep the first and last month's rent. I wasn't sure how long this would take." She sat up straight.

"I guess money talks." He tossed the chicken on

top of two rice piles and then took the beans out of the steamer. "Let's eat."

When she inhaled, her stomach turned, but it also begged for food. "Thanks for leaving out all the extra spices." Picking at her food, she forced herself to eat most of it. She knew she needed it. "Have you talked to your brother?" She looked up at him.

He stood with his plate in his hand, leaning against the kitchen sink. "The whole family is going to Adam's baseball game. Can't say Kamy's too thrilled. The only major problem is the dance on the *Minnie Ha Ha* this weekend." He stuffed his mouth full of food.

"Why let her go?"

"My point exactly, but they don't want Jessica running scared."

"Can Jake help?"

"He's already on it."

"What if they pin this on Craig?"

Splat.

His fork hit the floor.

"Enough dodging. What the hell was going on with you and Steve?" He picked up the fork and vigorously washed it and his plate.

"He knows I'm Jane Doe." Forcing herself to stand, she folded her arms across her chest.

Travis wiped his hands on the dishtowel. "How? And why the hell would he care?"

"Don't know, but he wants to talk to me tonight.

He said he'd stop by around eight." She separated her legs, then pushed her shoulder blades together, determined to hold her ground.

"What does your gut tell you?" Travis tossed the towel and moved closer.

This confused her. She was ready for a fight. She'd expected him to freak out.

"You heard the inflection in Jeff's voice?" she questioned.

He nodded.

"Put a dark wig on him, a mustache, and he's the man who raped me." She held her breath. Hearing her own admittance sent a cold shiver up her spine.

Travis leaned his hip on the counter and looked deep in thought. "Steve was accused of sexual harassment in Buffalo. He requested this office when he asked for a transfer." Travis looked at his wristwatch when a knock came at the door. "Answer it."

She let out all the air in her lungs in a big puff as she moved like a snail to the door. Whatever Steve wanted to share with her, she was glad Travis was going to be in the same room.

"Hi, Steve. Come in." The swirling of her stomach made her lightheaded, and her brow broke out in a cold sweat.

"I tried Travis, but he's not home," Steve said, looking very uncomfortable.

"That's because I'm right here." Travis took his

cell from the counter. "Damn silent mode. Sorry." He hooked it back to his hip.

An awkward silence filled the room. It stifled her breathing, and she felt like she got the wind knocked out of her.

Steve fiddled with a file and glanced between the two of them. "I'm really sorry about what happened to you." There was an unmistakable sincerity to his voice. "I may be extremely old-fashioned in my views about the world, but what Wilcox did to you is unforgivable."

Shauna's mouth opened, but only a faint gasp came out.

"Care to explain how you know all this?" Travis said, taking a step toward Steve. "Specifically, Wilcox."

"This might help." A folder shook in Steve's hand as he passed it to Travis.

Shauna glanced at the name written on the tab. "This is one of the earlier victims. But Travis couldn't make a connection. This case is still unsolved."

Steve rubbed his hand across his face. "My cousin."

Shauna exchanged a shocked glance with Travis.

"Why didn't you say anything to me?" Travis flipped through the file. "It's not like I kept my sister's murder a secret."

"I don't know. I guess I wasn't sure about

everything, until Shauna showed up." Steve shook his head. "My cousin had been missing for six months before she was found. We think she had been turning tricks. Drugs. You name it. But she didn't deserve this."

Shauna squeezed Steve's arm and then got a couple of sodas, handing them to everyone. "How do you know it's Jeff?" Shauna tried to mentally control the gurgling of her insides. They were so close, and she wouldn't back down—or break down.

Not now.

Not ever again.

"Your friend Jake's been asking a lot of questions. He just happened to ask my nephew who works here as a city cop. I put it together from there." He took a long sip of his soda. "I meant nothing by what I said to those women agents. I'm just not comfortable working with…"

"Well, you're just going to have to get over it. I'm not going anywhere, and I think the three of us need to figure out a way to help Jeff hang himself." She took a deep breath, feeling a renewed strength. One way or another Jeff Wilcox was going to pay for what he did.

"Say one thing out of line, and so help me, I'll hurt you." Travis shot Steve a dirty look.

"Knock it off." Shauna narrowed her eyes. "I can take care of myself."

"I bet you can." Steve laughed, slapping Travis on the back. "One of you is gonna have to quit when this is all over."

"You have the wrong impression," Shauna said with a clenched jaw.

"Really?" Steve lifted a brow. "I'll have to stay in the background. If I get all chummy with you two, he will suspect something. Does he know who you are?"

Shauna tried to hide her fear, but her body disobeyed her and shook.

He gave her an understanding look. Oddly, it made her feel better. "It won't be too long. I'll continue to monitor his movements. Keep your cell phone on." He shook Travis's hand and then faced Shauna, taking her by the shoulders. "I still don't think women belong in this line of work. You'll never change my mind about that, but I have a lot of respect for you. You've got some guts."

"Thanks."

After walking him to the door, she leaned up against it and rested her eyes. This had to end. She was sick and tired of being sick and tired all the time.

Oh my God. I can't be.

"Shit." She opened her eyes in shock of her own thoughts.

"What?" Travis stood in front of her, with a stupid, concerned look on his face.

"Nothing." She pushed him aside.

He took her by the arm and cocked his head.

"Okay, everything!" she snapped. "I hate this. I don't want to have to face him tomorrow. I want to crawl in a hole until…"

He rubbed her chin with his thumb, looking like he cared.

But who did he care about?

Her?

Or Jane Doe?

"No, you don't. You're a fighter, and we'll nail his ass. I promise." His warm lips gently glided across hers.

It caught her breath short, then he pulled her closer to him.

"No," she whispered, stepping back. "I can't. We can't." She crossed her arms around herself.

He scowled, placing his hands on his hips.

"Shauna, I feel things for you I haven't felt in years."

"It's just because we've been in an extreme situation."

"This isn't a movie. This is real life." He took a step closer, and she dodged him. "Are you trying to tell me you don't care about me?"

Of course she did. "It's not that simple." She did the math in her head, and she was most definitely a week or so late. Well, she wouldn't tell him until she was sure. And Jeff Wilcox was where he belonged.

"What's going on inside that pretty little head of yours?" He tapped his long index finger at her temple.

"You win."

"Win what?" He cocked a brow.

"I'll go out with you when this is over. A real date."

"We already established that." He took in a deep breath, like he was frustrated and losing his patience.

"But back off until then. I think you might be the one to change your mind."

He picked up her purse. "I won't be backing out. Let's get back to my place."

She followed him to his pickup, making sure no one was around to see her leave. They wanted Jeff, if he was watching, to think she was staying alone in her place.

---

*T*he next couple of days went by in a haze for Shauna. She and Travis were busy planning a trap for Jeff.

Jeff seemed to be aware that he was being watched, because he did nothing. He came to work, and then went to a half-empty apartment, not leaving until morning—as far as they could tell. There hadn't been another murder, which told the world the police had nabbed their man—the wrong man.

Shauna continued to have stomach issues. Travis

seemed to have lost his appetite as well. Obviously for different reasons.

Then there was this dance his niece was going to this weekend. Neither of them wanted her to go, but she had to trust that everyone in on this case right now would help take care of Jessica. The timing of the plan became very apparent to Shauna. They had to try to confront him on the night of the dance. The night that Jessica would be out of her parents' sight and possibly in harm's way.

---

*L*eaving the office on Friday evening, Shauna's entire body ached with the knowledge she might actually have to be alone with the man who'd raped her.

"Are you ready for this?" Travis asked as he pulled out of the federal building parking lot. A slight breeze ruffled the treetops, and the gray clouds threatened to release rain.

She took in a deep breath. "I'm ready to end this." She didn't look at him when he tugged at her phone on her hip.

"It's time."

She swallowed, feeling her throat close and then gasp for air as she dialed Jeff's phone number. Taking the hand Travis offered, she squeezed as hard as she could. She needed every ounce of strength she could muster from the both of them.

"Wilcox here," he answered in his normal voice.

"It's Shauna." Her hand shook as she tried to hold the phone to her ear. Flashes of him touching her, laughing at her, hurting her, tormented her brain.

"Well, hello." His voice changed and rattled her to the point of near panic.

She closed her eyes, feeling her stomach fly up her throat. "We need to talk," she heard herself say.

"Really, 'bout what?"

About your funeral, you sick bastard. "Work stuff." That was real professional. "I need some information about Nagel."

"I thought you knew all about Nagel." His tone rang sadistic in her ears.

"I wish. The cops have too many holes. I still don't think it's him. That file of yours had some interesting information; mind if I take another look?"

Silence on the other end.

Travis held her hand, stroking her skin with his thumb. The safety of his touch allowed her to maintain some sense of control.

"Jeff?" she questioned.

"Sorry, just looking for that file you want to *fish* through. Why didn't you just drop by my office before you left?"

"Travis thinks I should leave it alone. He's satisfied the cops have the right guy."

"Okay. You've *hooked* me. When do you want to meet?"

"How about in an hour and a half. I'll meet you at Capri's."

"I'll see you there. Goodbye, Shauna," he said in the voice that made her tremble in fear. The way her name echoed across the phone sent her stomach on another roll.

She flipped the phone shut, praying she wouldn't have to have Travis pull over. Being sick again would only complicate matters more. Not that the reason for her being sick didn't complicate things enough.

Closing her eyes, she rested her head against the window. She could hear the slight pitter-patter of the rain as it hit the glass next to her ear.

She jumped, feeling the door open.

"Come on, sweetheart." Travis lifted her into his arms.

"No," she whispered.

"I just talked with Steve. Jeff's at his apartment."

She relaxed into Travis's body, unaware she had been asleep. She was so tired. It was just the case. Her job. She tried to remind herself, knowing that a small entity was draining her of all her energy. She felt something soft adjust to her weight. "Have you forgiven Gina for what she did?"

"Forgiven her?" He pinched his brow. "I suppose." His voice was flat and unemotional.

"I mean, could you go on with your life? Have a family with someone else?"

"She's not why I gave up on the idea of having a

family, not entirely." The couch lifted under her as he sat down next to her, pushing her head into his lap. "Gina and I had problems before she had the abortion. Looking back, the only reason I wanted to marry her was because she was pregnant. I'm not sure I really loved her like a husband is supposed to, and she wanted me to give up on finding Marie's killer. She said I was obsessed."

Shauna took in a deep breath. "You are."

Travis cleared his throat. "I want a family someday. But I want it to be because I'm in love, not solely because of a baby. I don't think it would be fair to bring someone into my mess."

His fingers stroked her hair, then tingled down her arm.

The soft touch of his skin made her want to curl up like a kitten in his lap and forget all about putting Wilcox away. His scent, which she could never really place, filled her lungs. It was manly, but there was that sensitiveness to him, even his smell. This was a man who loved deeply.

But could he love her? The real her.

Deep down she knew he'd love his child and be there for him or her. But she couldn't be in a loveless marriage. She wouldn't marry a man only because she carried his child, and she didn't think Travis could love her for her.

"And I've only thought about family stuff lately. Before, I pretty much stayed away from women."

Opening her eyes, she sat up and searched his. "I don't believe that. You're the kind of guy women flock to."

That caught a throaty laugh. "I don't put myself out there. The women I've dated over the last few years haven't been the marrying type." His hand ran down the back of her head, sending a warm glow all through her body.

She felt safe and cared for. But who did he really care about? "No serious girlfriends since her?"

He shook his head. "In the beginning, I was too upset. I took it out on all women. Then I decided to stay away from the intellectual type, until recently." His smile was playful.

"You mean women who have a plan."

He shrugged.

"I have a plan." She pulled away. Even though he said he didn't want marriage because of a baby, she knew him well enough to know he'd demand it.

"Really?" He leaned back on the armrest of the sofa, still with that playful smile plastered on his face. She wanted to stuff her foot in his mouth, better yet, *his* foot.

To her mortification, she let out a little chuckle.

He lifted his leg and put it on her lap, nudging her ribs. "The plan?"

"Oh, yeah. Go to Quantico, work with you, catch a killer and then, catch a few more." She took his foot in her hand.

"You can do that here, you know?"

"I've got to move on. Too much of the past here."

"That's bullshit." He yanked his foot from her hand, squirming.

She grabbed it back.

"Stop." He wiggled on the couch, laughing. "Revenge is something I do well." He lifted both brows.

She released his foot for the moment. Tucking her feet under her behind, she welcomed both his feet in her lap. "Someday I'd like to go to work at the national office."

"What about being a wife and mother?" His stare was so intense, her breath caught.

"I've never really thought about it. Trusting a man with my whole heart isn't something I've spent any time considering, and I like my job." She had to admit to herself, though, that she did trust Travis. Her heart pounded so heavy and fast, she thought for sure he could hear it. "Besides, I always worry about the possible hereditary factors in child abuse and alcoholism."

"That's about the dumbest thing I've ever heard you say. You, my sweet, would make a wonderful mother. You're kind, loving, and generous, and it would be a privilege to be loved by you."

End of conversation.

"Well, I'm not the settling down type." She picked up his feet and pushed them to the floor. "We need to go." She rose from the couch and moved as fast as she could toward the door. She didn't want to talk anymore. Why she'd even brought it up she would never know.

Except that they might be having a child together.

15

Travis tapped his watch with his index finger and then held it to his ear. Jeff was late, but Jeff was good at being late. It seemed the only thing he was ever on time for was court, and only by a hair.

Travis opened the door to his pickup and got out. He needed to stretch his legs. It was almost eight, and Jeff should have been at Capri's a half hour ago.

Something's not right.

He flipped open his cell phone and dialed Steve's number. "Damn it." He got his voicemail. Cracking his knuckles, he decided to go in the restaurant. This being one of his favorite spots, it wouldn't be unheard of for him to just show up for a beer. Besides, he didn't like the idea of Shauna being in there all alone.

Entering the bar and grill, he scanned the room. Nothing out of place. Bonnie waved and pointed to the corner booth in the back. Shauna had eyed him the moment he'd pushed open the door, but she didn't look too happy to see him.

"What the hell are you doing?" A scowl formed across her pretty face.

"Steve's not answering," he said as Bonnie brought him a diet cola with lemon. "I don't like this."

Fear flickered behind her cool-blue eyes. "You should go check on him."

"Not without you." He squeezed his lemon and stirred his drink.

"I need to wait here in case Jeff shows." She swallowed, looking over Travis's shoulder at someone entering the bar.

He followed her stare, but it was just another patron. "We stay together."

Silence followed.

Travis chewed on a piece of ice and tossed a ten on the table, glancing at his watch. "He's up to something. It's been too long. I think we need to go."

"Where?"

"To find Steve," Travis said. "Or Lake George. Hell if I know."

No sooner were they in the car and driving down New Scotland Avenue than his phone rang. "Brown here," he answered.

"Is this Travis Brown?" a female voice asked.

"Who is this?" He glanced at Shauna.

"My name is Cilla Regal. I'm a nurse at Albany

Medical Center. Steve Ramsey asked that I give you a call. He said it was important."

Travis pulled the truck to the side of the road with the intention to turn around and head to the hospital. "What happened?"

"He's been shot and said it was important that you knew."

"Shit. Is he okay?" Travis glanced at Shauna, whose body paled.

"He just went into surgery so we can remove the bullet, but he ranted that I had to call you. I really have to go."

"Did he say anything else?"

"Just that you would understand the situation."

"Thanks." He clicked his phone closed and dropped his head to the steering wheel. "Steve's been shot."

"Jessica," Shauna whispered.

Travis stiffened his back, lurching upright. Fear tore open his heart. For the first time in a long while, he had no idea what to do.

A warm hand squeezed his bicep. "Call Jake." Her voice was soft, but commanding.

He looked at her. Tears welled in her eyes as she released his cell phone from his grasp. He continued to stare into her all-knowing eyes as she continued to press numbers on his cell phone.

"It's ringing." She handed the phone to him, pulling out her own.

The next few moments went by in a haze. He could barely piece together what had happened. Shauna called Scott, who had been informed of the shooting. Travis heard her tell Scott what they suspected, along with who she was.

But the conversation with Jake sent him into a fit of rage. He had to have Jake repeat the words twice. "The *Minnie Ha Ha* caught fire, Kirk was knocked unconscious, and Jessica is missing," ripped through his veins like lava flowing from a volcano.

He flung open the truck door with such force that it slammed shut, barely missing his hand. "Damn it!" He tossed his cell phone to the curb, shattering it to pieces. Uttering numerous curses, he kicked and pounded on his truck.

"Travis!" Shauna shouted. "Get ahold of yourself."

He snapped his head in her direction. She stood about two feet from him with her hands firmly planted on her hips.

"This isn't helping," she said softly.

"Where did he take her?" Blinded by rage, he took her by the shoulders and shook her. "Damn it! Where did he take her?" he repeated, letting his anger and fear get the best of him. He didn't think his family could go through this again.

He couldn't go through this again.

"I don't know," she said. She just stood there, letting him shake her. "A fishing pole," she muttered.

"What?" His body froze, and he stared at her.

She blinked, then shook her head. "I see a fishing pole."

"Have you cracked?"

"In the corner of the room, when I awoke, I saw a fishing pole. I didn't think anything of it. *God.* He asked me if I wanted to *fish* through his file. He said I *hooked* him."

"Talk to me," Travis demanded.

"I assumed I was in a hotel room. It looked like one. A bed, a dresser, and a bathroom. I also assumed I was south of Albany since that was the direction of the train. But what if I was at the—"

"Cabin on the Hudson," he finished her thought for her. "The article said who owned it." He cracked his neck and turned from her, trying desperately to remember who owned the cabin.

---

*F*or Shauna, who owned the cabin didn't matter. Getting to the cabin did. She sat in the passenger seat, gripping the holy shit bar as if she were in a sports car. But not because of his driving. He didn't drive fast enough for her taste.

He maneuvered in and out of traffic with ease as he barked out orders and suggestions to his boss and anyone else who would listen. "I'm getting the damn runaround." He clicked her phone closed and honked the horn.

"What does Scott say?"

"Go by the book." He must have hit the gas as the truck pitched forward, speeding past the white SUV that finally got the hint.

"Who's been called?" Shauna wondered how much of her theory was being taken seriously. Scott seemed to take her words as fact, but he didn't seem thrilled by her confession. Actually, he got downright nasty.

"Locals and state police." Travis hit the steering wheel, jerking the truck to the side. "Damn it. If you had only told me who you were from the beginning."

She recoiled at the truth in his words, praying another victim wouldn't have to suffer all because she never had the courage to come forward. All because she couldn't identify the man who'd raped her.

Her cell phone rang.

She looked at it and then handed it to Travis without saying a word. She listened as he talked with Scott, but none of it mattered. They were going to be too late. And she was to blame.

The truck slowed to a stop next to an unmarked car and three other local cop cars. Travis rolled down the window as she scanned the scene and knew this would be her chance to make sure no more young girls died at the hands of Jeff Wilcox.

"Agent Brown?" A large man approached the truck.

Travis nodded.

"I'm Detective Howard with the State Police. All the lights are off, no car. I've got three men in place." Detective Howard pointed to the trees and somewhere across the yard, but Shauna didn't see anyone. "I understand your niece is a possible hostage. This is your call." He stood tall, holding his hand up to the locals to remain where they were.

Travis got out of his truck and scanned the area. "This is my partner, Agent Morgan." His tone was professional and completely detached.

Shauna felt the bile rise slowly up her throat. She swallowed, shaking the detective's hand, and then pulled away from the two men, who started talking about a plan. Her blood raced through her veins, and before she really knew what she was thinking, she was on her belly, making her way toward the cabin.

Her pulse beat wildly, but her mind worked slowly and with meticulous care. She had to find a way in. She crept under a bush, and for the first time she saw two of the three policemen. They were well hidden, and it was going to be difficult to get past them. But she had to.

She felt around on the ground, searching for something to toss. She just needed to get across the small yard and land herself on the riverside.

The rock she tossed bounced on the ground with

a few quiet thuds. The two cops looked at each other, and then one slinked in the direction of the noise while the other backed him up. Without thinking, she was on her feet, running toward the front of the house. Just as she rounded the corner...

Someone grabbed her.

"Hello, my kitten."

Shauna blinked. Jeff's hand covered her mouth as he yanked her into the cabin. She shifted her gaze, looking around the small cabin. *Where's Jessica?* She wiggled, trying to break free.

"Still the feisty little feline, I see." He opened a door.

Jessica sat in a chair, bound and gagged and looking scared to death. Shauna had to break free. She stomped on his foot.

"Damn, bitch." Jeff tossed her in a chair and pointed a gun in her face. "Don't do it." He took her weapon from her hands and tossed it on the bed.

"Let her go, Jeff. You've got me." Shauna glanced at Jessica and tried to comfort her with a slight smile.

Jeff snorted. "What makes you think I want used trash like you?" He ran his hand down Jessica's cheek. "She's still young and innocent."

"Still?" Shauna hadn't meant to express her thought out loud.

He laughed. "I had so been hoping to save her soul, but you and your dickhead boyfriend put a damper on my party. Looks like Travis grew a brain."

Shauna's skin prickled as he ran the cold butt of the gun down the side of her face. "Put your hands behind your back."

"You won't get away with this." She did as he instructed, praying Travis and his newfound friend had their plan all formulated. "Travis won't wait outside for long."

"No, I guess he won't. The question is who will he save?" He pulled the rope tight around her wrists and then started working on her feet. "His lover? Or his niece?"

"Why are you doing this?" Shauna found herself wanting all the answers.

He threw his head back and laughed. "God, those office shrinks would have a field day with me." His face was inches from hers, and his breath felt cold against her skin.

She forced herself to look into the depths of hell. "Tell me," she demanded.

He let out a little breath. "I snapped." An eerie smile broadened his face. "I watched my girlfriend sneak out of her house to go meet someone else."

"So you followed them and killed her?"

His eyes narrowed. "That would be the textbook case." He rubbed his jaw. "But that's not quite what happened."

"What happened, Jeff?" She used his name in hopes of keeping things personal and buying her some time.

"If you must know, Shelly, my girlfriend, had been saving herself for me. We were going to do it the night of the prom."

"But she ran out on you and did it with someone else?"

"Shut up!" He smashed the butt of the gun into Shauna's cheek.

Blood dripped down her face, and her eye throbbed. Glancing at a wide-eyed Jessica, Shauna lifted her chin. No way would he make her fall to pieces. "Did you find them together?"

"No."

Shauna stared down at his gun, pointing at her face. "Then what happened?"

"She must have met him sometime before the prom. She was no virgin when I got ahold of her."

"Wait, you have no proof she was cheating on you?" Not that it mattered, but as long as he kept on talking, she'd keep asking.

"She didn't bleed. It wasn't painful, and her body rocked with mine like she'd been doing it forever. She even suggested how we do it. When I confronted her, she just told me she watched a few movies and played with herself. I didn't believe her, so I killed her."

"Just like that." Shauna swallowed.

"No, not just like that. We fought. She tried to tell me all sorts of lies, but I knew the truth. My mother showed me."

"What?" Shauna felt her eyes widen. "What did your mother do to you?" she whispered.

"She showed me how a virgin wouldn't behave."

The gun pointed in Shauna's face shook. His finger wiggled against the trigger. Sweat dripped down the side of her face. Jess whimpered and struggled.

"Jesus," Shauna muttered, understanding the complexity of the situation. "Where's your mother now?"

"Where all the other lost souls are." He tucked his gun in his pants and pulled out some duct tape. "Hell." He slapped the tape across her mouth. "I think you're about to meet your maker, Shauna."

She held his gaze, knowing she'd die, but somehow she knew Travis would find a way in and save Jessica. Shauna shifted her gaze to see the young girl. Tears streaked down her face. Quietly, Shauna thanked God she'd been able to save Jessica from the same fate her aunt had faced. Shauna would die knowing Jeff's reign as the "Princess Killer" was about to end. Travis and his family would be able to move forward and live out their lives in peace.

Travis would be able to let go of the past and find someone to share his wonderful, kind heart with. A single tear fell to her lap. There'd been a moment or two she had thought she might be that woman. She breathed slowly, in and out, and waited.

"**S**hit," Travis spat when he turned to ask Shauna a question. "Damn you." He raked his hand through his hair.

"What's up?" Detective Howard asked.

Travis twisted his head, then twisted it again, but his neck wouldn't crack. He nodded in the direction of the house.

"She wouldn't?" Howard blinked, looking at Travis as if he were nuts. "And I thought I had to worry about you going off half-cocked. Not her."

"This is personal for her, too," Travis said. "This isn't going to happen. I've searched too many damn years for you, Shauna," Travis said under his breath.

"What do you want to do?" Howard asked.

"I'm going in." He shrugged and took out his weapon, then checked it over. "The only way you will stop me is to shoot me." He didn't look back, just put one foot in front of the other, and in the open, he followed the stone path to the front of the house. Standing at the front door, he took in a deep breath. "I'm coming in, Wilcox." He turned the handle, held his gun out in front, and entered the small cabin.

Since the sun had already set, his eyes didn't need time to adjust to the darkness, but his nose needed time to adjust to the smell. The stench almost choked him. When he swallowed, he could taste dead fish.

With the door to his back, he scanned the room.

To the right, a wooden couch with a sailboat lamp sat under the window. To the left, there was a kitchen table, a stovetop, and a sink. Ahead were two closed doors. One had to be the bedroom; the other he assumed was a bathroom.

He took one last look around the room to ensure he wouldn't get jumped from behind as he took small steps toward the door. This time he remained silent. He cocked his head to the side, listening.

Nothing.

He reached out, clutching the door handle to the right. At the last minute, he decided to go with the door on the left. In one swift motion, he threw back the door, weapon drawn, and sucked in as much oxygen as he could.

"You bastard," he cursed.

"Welcome to the party. Looks like I get to go out with some style." Wilcox smiled as he waved his gun from Shauna to Jessica.

Both of them sat bound and gagged in chairs. Jessica was crying and pale. Shauna was eerily calm.

"You're gonna die, Wilcox," Travis held his gun, pointed right between his eyes. Killing a man never seemed so damned enjoyable.

"I know. Ain't life grand? But who will you save?" Wilcox lowered his gun and pointed it in Shauna's face. "So pretty. And a good fuck, too." He licked her cheek, then took his gun to Jessica's temple. "But she's so innocent. I just wish I could have been her first, her only."

Travis forced his eyes to hold focus as he tried to calm his trembling hands. He held the trigger so tight, he was actually afraid he might shoot. Shooting at the wrong time would cost one of them their lives. Not something he was prepared to live with. What the hell was Howard up to outside?

"Only one way in this place," Jeff said as if he could read Travis's mind. "God, this is great. When I heard she was coming here, I came right there in my pants. And to think, I had her before you did. That must kill you."

The anger coursing through Travis's body tensed his muscles to the point of pain. He'd never, not in his entire life, felt pure hatred in his heart. Not something he ever wanted to feel again.

A scratching noise caught his attention, and he glanced toward Shauna. Her eyes shifted toward her feet and then back to meet his.

He wanted to smile but couldn't give his hand to Jeff. Shauna would know the right moment to make her move.

"I'm going to make sure you rot in hell, Wilcox." Travis shifted, and Shauna jolted her body forward.

Crack. Thud!

Shauna's chair crashed forward, and Travis kicked his leg up, knocking Jeff's gun from his hand, but Jeff reached for something behind his back. "Don't move!" Travis yelled, but Jeff moved.

Pop!

"Jesus! You shot me, you asshole!" Jeff screamed, dropping to the floor, holding his blown kneecap.

"Hold it right there." Travis kicked Jeff in the chest as he tried to get up. "Move again and it will be considered self-defense. A few counseling sessions and my conscience would be clear." He stepped down hard on Jeff's chest, looking him in the eye.

Nothing human lurked behind his cloudy, gray stare. The man was as cold as the dead fish on the kitchen table. Travis narrowed his eyes, moving the gun closer to the small space above his nose. The urge to shoot surged through him with such force, he didn't recognize himself.

"Agent Brown." The stern voice behind him made him back off. He blinked, realizing this soulless man looking up at him wasn't worth it.

"Read him his rights and help me get Shauna and my niece untied." Gingerly, Travis took the gag off his young, trembling niece. She sobbed uncontrollably as he removed her bindings and took her into his arms.

"Shh, baby. It's over now." He stroked her hair. "I have to check on Shauna."

"I'm fine," Shauna said softly, rubbing her wrists. A sense of sadness engulfed her eyes as she turned from him.

"Let's get both of them checked out." Detective

Howard placed a hand on Shauna's elbow and guided her out the door as another officer read Jeff his rights and handcuffed him.

Travis lifted his niece in his arms and carried her out of the death-filled cabin. Not only had the stench grabbed a hold of him, he'd also almost succumbed to his deepest fear. He'd wanted to kill Jeff.

An ambulance waited down the road, along with a dozen agents, a few locals, the state police, Jake, and his brother Bill.

A half hour passed as Travis and Shauna gave their stories, separately. Standard procedure. Jessica was reunited with her parents, physically unharmed. When all should be well, Travis saw his world come crashing down.

"Are you okay?" he asked Shauna, helping her down from the back of the ambulance. He touched the bruise on her blood-streaked face.

"I thought I would feel different." She hugged herself, pulling away from him.

"So did I," he admitted and tried to take her in his arms. He'd spent so many years searching for this one man. The feeling of capturing him had been anticlimactic. His only real thoughts were with all the innocent victims who might be able to rest in peace.

And his aching heart.

She stepped back, eyeing him suspiciously. "I have to put this part of my life behind me." Her eyes were welling with tears.

"Don't push me away." Everything seemed to be moving in slow motion. "We need to talk."

"No." She put up her hands and stared at him with extreme resolve in her eyes.

"I understand how hard this has been for you, but just give it some time."

"You understand nothing. I need to end this chapter now. All of it, including you."

He opened his mouth to say something, but the officer coming up behind Shauna spoke first.

"Can I give anyone a lift?" the sheriff asked.

"Please." For a brief moment, she stared at Travis.

He was unable to say the words flooding his mind. No matter what he thought, or felt, he was still Marie's brother. Every time Shauna looked at him, she would be reminded of what had happened.

"Goodbye," she said softly, then turned and walked off with the sheriff.

He stood on the lonely road and watched the last police car roll away, with Shauna in it. She'd opted to get a ride home from a perfect stranger. Clear as the moon in the sky, she didn't love him.

"Why me?" He tossed his hands wide, staring up at the heavens. Angrily, he wiped the tears that stained his face. Knowing she'd never turn around and fight for something that didn't exist for her. He hopped in his pickup and prayed for the light of day.

16

The following morning, Shauna lay in her bed and stared at the ceiling. It would take a few moments before she could make herself move without throwing up. She blinked, then blinked again. She should be happy. She could finally put her past behind her for good and move on to something brighter.

She had nothing to fear for the first time in her pathetic existence, yet she was truly afraid. Not of being harmed, but of being alone. Before, her loneliness stemmed from her desire to make sure a killer was put behind bars.

Well, Jeff Wilcox was on his way to hell. Just as she got home, Scott called to tell her Jeff had tried to escape, and the police had to shoot him again. She suspected that's what he'd wanted all along.

With great care, she lifted her covers and rolled to the side. Her stomach gurgled. "Crap." She flew from her bed, making a beeline for the bathroom. Staring down into the depths of her toilet as an empty stomach attempted to squeeze out nothing, she knew the pregnancy test that sat on her kitchen counter was now a reality. She had to take it.

"Okay, plus sign, you talk to him; negative, you don't." She filled the little drip thing with her sample and then walked away. She found herself flipping through the channels as the three minutes ticked by. Then four. Then five.

Unable to put it off any longer, she padded to the bathroom and snatched the test. "Damn." A big plus sign filled the results window. If she didn't tell him, she would be no different than Gina. Well, she was better than that.

She wouldn't get rid of the baby. The timing couldn't be worse, but she loved the baby, and she loved its father.

She wouldn't marry him. Loving him had nothing to do with it. His damned nobility had everything to do with it. He would probably do the dinner and roses thing. Get all sappy, all for the sake of putting on a good front.

But Travis didn't love her.

It was okay that he went for his niece first. That was the right thing to do. She was his flesh and blood. But even after all the commotion had settled down, he had seemed distant. He didn't really try to touch her. She didn't let him, and he didn't push it. Actually, he'd backed off immediately, even letting her walk away into the night with another man. A man in love would fight, especially Travis.

So why was she in such a damn hurry to shower, change, and jump in her borrowed car? Hell if she knew, but it had to be done. Her pulse picked up speed as she pulled off the Northway and headed toward Travis's parents' house. Scott had told her that he had headed up there for a few days.

Her stomach flipped as she pulled in right behind his pickup. She didn't know what she was going to say, or how she was going to say it, but she needed to be strong. She took a deep breath and knocked fiercely at the door.

After filling his family in on all the sordid details, the last thing Travis expected was his mother's lecture on how to treat a lady, but that is exactly what she did. Then his father piped in, and even little Kamy told him he was a real stinker.

The following morning, he sat out on the dock, alone. He sipped his coffee, wondering how to approach Shauna. He needed to talk to her. Apologize and beg for forgiveness if necessary. No point in denying it, he loved her. He wondered what she would have done if he had chased after her last night.

He had no idea what she felt for him, but running away from this part of her life wasn't the answer.

"Hey, Uncle Trav." Jessica appeared next to him.

"Hi, precious." He took her by the hand and pulled her down on the dock next to him.

"You haven't called me that since I was nine." She smiled sweetly. Almost like nothing had happened.

He touched her bruised face. "I'm so sorry, Jessica."

"I know." She took his hand. "I was so scared. He knew all about Aunt Marie, and Shauna, and you. He said he killed Kirk." The tears formed in her eyes.

"Kirk's fine. Your mom and dad are going to let you visit him today."

She smiled like the kid she was. "Really?! They told you that?" She squirmed.

"Shh, it's our secret." He kissed her cheek, amazed by her resilience.

"There you are." His mother sat down, taking Jessica by the hand and dangling her feet in the water. "Your parents are looking for you, dear. I think they have a surprise for you."

Jessica jumped. "Thanks, Grandma!" She planted a kiss on her grandmother and then giggled as she scurried away.

"You'd never know she had nightmares all night." His mother looked out over the lake.

"That may happen for a while," he said, solemnly.

"Here." She held out a small box.

"What's this?"

"Grandma's engagement ring." A tear fell from her eye, landing in the lake.

Everything happens for a reason. "That was meant for Marie." He squeezed the box, refusing to open it.

"It was meant for the youngest living grandchild." She pushed it under his nose.

"I can't." He stood. "That ring was meant for Marie." He repeated with defiance.

"Now it will be Shauna's." With dignity, his mother rose and stood inches from him, her face lined with love and determination.

"She doesn't love me. She wants to shut the door on the past, on us, on me. Save it for Jessica, or even Kamy." He tried to turn from her, but a stern hand squeezed his forearm.

His mother narrowed her eyes. "Marie would want her to have it."

"You're not listening to me, Mother."

"Because you're not making any sense! Have you told her you love her? You do love her, don't you?"

"Yeah, I do," he admitted.

"Then you have to tell her." She shoved the box in his hand. "At least tell her and give her the chance to deny it."

She turned on her heels and gasped. "Travis," she whispered.

"What's the matter? Mom?" he questioned, staring at her flushed face.

"She's here." His mom gently tugged his ear, smiled, and then glided up the stairs.

He froze. Unable to move. His pulse quickened as he looked up toward the house. There stood the woman he loved.

His equal.

His life partner.

He shoved the box in his denim shorts and blinked. He shook his head, trying to clear his thoughts and find the right words, the perfect words. He cleared his throat as she approached.

"Hi, Travis." She made eye contact.

"I love you," he blurted out like a moron.

"Say what?" She stared at him like he was a total idiot.

"I mean…umm…oh, Christ, what the hell. I love you, Shauna Morgan, and I want to be your partner forever." He pulled the box from his pocket, and with trembling hands he took out his grandmother's engagement ring. "Marry me?"

He took her hand, kissed it, and looked at her. "God, would you say something? Anything?"

She opened her mouth but only gasped as he slid the ring on her finger.

"Was that a yes?"

She nodded and threw her arms around his shoulders. "Yes." She kissed him.

But he wasn't prepared for the onslaught, and he tumbled backward.

Splash!

"Shauna." He came up from the chilly waters, searching, but she was…

Splat.

She popped up, squirting water in his face.

"You little brat. Get over here." He found her arm and yanked her to him. "Tell me." He kissed her lips once.

"What?" She smiled, her eyes sparkling in the sunlight.

He tugged her toward the dock and helped her up. "Tell me." He pushed down on her back, putting his full weight on her.

"Do I have to?" She smiled devilishly.

"If you don't, I'll have to take the ring back." He lifted her hand, admiring the sparkling diamond that was almost as bright as her smile.

"When did you get this?"

"It was my grandmother's. She used to tell me that everything happened for a reason. I never believed her, until now. My mother just gave it to me right before you showed up. Why are you here, anyway?" He pulled his head back and stared at her.

"Your grandmother's?" she whispered. She threaded her fingers through his hair. "I love you." She looked beyond his eyes to his soul and touched the deepest part of him. "I love you," she whispered through her tears.

"Don't cry, sweetheart." The water dripping from her eyes tugged at his heartstrings.

"I can't help it. Your grandmother's ring? I don't think I'm good enough."

He brushed his thumb across the purple mark below her eye. "I promise to love you every day I breathe." He kissed her, barely touching his lips against hers. Then, abruptly he pulled back. "Why did you come here today?" he questioned. His curiosity was going to get him in trouble.

Her face brightened in the morning sun. "Mostly, because I love you." She cupped his face.

"I love you back." He lowered his lips to hers in what he intended to be a promissory kiss, but it quickly got out of hand. Her lips were soft and sweet under his. Her tongue rushed forward, eagerly searching for the warmth of his and sent his reasoning tumbling into the water.

"Now that's what I call sucking face," Adam yelled from the porch. "Ouch, Grandma!" Adam yelped.

"Get your butt back in this house right now, young man," Bill barked. "Give them some privacy."

Travis, as gracefully as he could muster, lifted Shauna to her feet. "I think we need to go face the firing squad."

She chuckled. "Ya think we might have surprised them just a little?"

"Nope." He took her by the hand and led her toward the house. His family seemed to expect them to end up together the moment she'd walked into his life.

When they entered the kitchen, his entire family stood there with smiles and just waited.

"Well?" Rita questioned.

"She said yes." Travis felt his heart flutter with the purest sense of joy he'd ever known.

"Well, I'll be damned." Bill laughed.

His mother placed her hands on Shauna's shoulder. "You bring a part of her back to me. I thank you for that, but mostly I thank you for letting this family love you, for you."

"I'm sorry—"

"Hush, child." His mother's finger pressed against her lips. "You have nothing to apologize for. Just make sure my son makes you happy." She took her in her arms.

Travis rubbed his eyes, hoping no one noticed his tears. The last thing he needed was to be teased once again. He waited as each member of his family hugged his fiancée. He smiled at the thought, then frowned. This could be interesting. His mother would actually be able to plan this wedding, and she knew it.

"Let's get these two lovebirds into some dry clothes and start planning this wedding. I have so many ideas. How about December? That should give us enough time. You'll make a beautiful winter bride…"

*S*hauna swallowed hard and tried to listen to Rita's babbling, but a December wedding? It was July. She would be fat by then. That was the last thing she wanted for her wedding. *Oh my God!* Was she totally out of her mind? She said yes when she promised herself she wouldn't cave to him, but noble he wasn't. Not this time. He loved her. She felt it right through to her core. But she still had one more secret to tell him, but this time she knew she'd make him happy.

"Shauna?" A warm tingle shot up her spine.

She smiled. "Hmm?" She looked at Travis.

"December? Any objections?" he whispered in her ear as they made their way into the kitchen from the front porch.

"I don't want a December wedding," she said a little too loudly, because the whole room quieted and stared at her.

"Goodness, I'm sorry. I got so carried away. What do you want, dear?" Rita put down her pen and gave her the mother look, the one she seemed to use to get her way.

Shauna cleared her throat. "I didn't mean to insult anyone. It's just that I…well, I really didn't want to wait. I mean, I don't have any family to speak of, and a big church wedding, well, the church would be pretty lopsided."

"You ain't kidding," Kim said.

"When and where do you want to get married?" Travis asked as he circled his wet arms around her chilled body, but she'd never felt so warm in her life.

She took a deep breath and looked around the room. "Within the next month and out there."

She pointed toward the lake.

"On the lake?" Rita questioned.

"On the sundeck and at dusk, just all of you. I'd like Jessica to be my maid of honor." Shauna looked around the room at all the smiling faces, realizing she'd just found home. The arms around her tightened, and warm soft lips pressed against her neck.

"Me? Really? Oh, that would be so cool!" Jessica jumped up from her seat and practically threw herself at Shauna.

"Well, now, we've got our work cut out for us, don't we? First, though, you must go get your future bride some dry clothes," Rita dictated, and the room followed.

Shauna was given some shorts and a T-shirt to change into. Standing alone in Travis's old room, she glanced at the bed. They had made love for the first time in that bed. She held her stomach. They might have even created their baby in that bed. She caught herself smiling. She held up her hand and gazed at her ring. "How the hell did this happen?"

Someone knocked at the door.

"Come in," Shauna called, feeling a little nervous all of a sudden.

"If I get out of control with this wedding, let me know. I just want you both to be happy." Rita came in with a very large box, placing it on the bed.

"Oh, I'm happy all right, but I'm sorry if I insulted you." Shauna looked into Rita's knowing eyes.

"I like to take care of my family." Rita gave Shauna a hug. "I've felt some kind of connection to you from the moment I laid eyes on you. I'd like to help with all the arrangements."

"Would you take me shopping for dresses?"

"I'd like nothing more, but only if you don't want to wear this." Rita tapped her finger on the box. "This was my wedding dress."

Shauna covered her mouth as Rita pulled the gown from the box. "Oh…this is perfect. You wouldn't mind?" She held the dress up to herself. It was a simple but elegant halter style gown with pearls lining the trim. It was exactly what she would have picked for herself.

"I'd be honored." Rita sniffed.

Shauna looked into the mirror. "God, it's beautiful. I would love to wear it." She tried to hide her tears, but it was impossible.

Rita stood behind Shauna, smiling. "You are going to make a beautiful bride…and a wonderful mother."

Shauna's eyes widened.

"It was just a guess." Rita leaned over her shoulder and kissed her cheek. "I take it he doesn't know yet?"

Unable to form words, Shauna shook her head.

Rita took Shauna by the shoulders and turned her, cupping her face. "I hurt when I think about what happened to you, to my Marie, but I thank God for bringing you here to us."

Another knock came at the door.

"Shauna?" Travis's voice vibrated through the wood door.

Shauna jumped. "Oh my God! He can't see this! It would be bad luck!" Frantically, she helped Rita put it in the box and shove it in the closet.

"Sentiment? From you?"

"Well. With some things," Shauna said.

"We'll pretend to go shopping, that way he won't know you're wearing my dress, and we can spend some time alone together." Rita opened the door and slipped out, but not before she tugged playfully at Travis's ear.

Travis smiled, closing the door behind him. "Whenever she does that, I've done something that's deserving of a lecture."

"You have." Shauna giggled. "God, I love you." She wrapped her arms around his strong, lean body. Never in her wildest dreams did she think she'd feel like she belonged somewhere.

"I love you, too." He clutched her hips and pushed back. "What's going on?" He shot her a pointed look. "I know you, and you're omitting something. I want to know what it is." He pulled her a little closer.

His hands applied warm pressure on her back; she arched into him.

"Ask me why I came here today."

"Why'd you come here today?" He tilted his head.

"I told myself that even when you offered marriage, I'd say no."

He scowled, pushing her back. "I don't follow."

"I know." She laughed, taking his hand and placing it on her stomach, under her T-shirt.

"If you love me, why wouldn't you want to marry me?" His brow lifted, and he searched her face for meaning.

"Because I thought you would want to marry me out of a sense of duty or something."

"What made you think I would propose in the first place?" His blue, sparkling eyes twinkled as the light bulb slowly flicked on in his brain. "Are you... pregnant?" He dropped his chin, his jaw gaping open.

"I am." She pressed her hand against his and smiled like she'd never smiled before.

"I think I need to sit down." He sat on the edge of the bed, rubbing his ear.

"Are you all right?"

He looked up at her with admiration in his eyes. "I'm a little stunned. A baby? Are you sure?"

She nodded.

He narrowed his eyes. "You told my mother."

"She tricked me." Shauna wiggled as Travis ran his fingers across her stomach. "Are you happy about the baby?"

He dropped his head to her stomach. "'Happy' doesn't do my feelings justice. This morning I was contemplating begging you just to go out on a date with me. Now we're getting married in a month and having a baby. Plus, I'm going to start a new job."

"You're really going to start your own P.I. business with Jake?"

"Yeah. Are you okay with that?"

"Why wouldn't I be?"

"I don't know. It's long, hard hours and dangerous."

"And your job now is different how?"

"Good point," he said. "What about your transfer?"

"Haven't asked for it yet."

"It's up to you, but I kind of like living here."

"I can work with that," she said.

"My whole adult life I've been looking for you." He chuckled. "Ironic, isn't it?"

She nodded.

"I only wish I could take all the pain and suffering of what happened to you away, but I'm so damned grateful you came back." His long fingers ran through her damp hair, and his eyes looked over her face with a loving humbleness only he could show. "You returned for me."

Thank you for taking the time to read Jane Doe's Return! Please feel free to leave an honest review. If you enjoyed this book, please check the second book in this series *The Butterfly Murders*.
You alos might enjoy my Legacy Series:

Dark Legacy
Legacy of Lies
Secret Legacy

Sign up for my Newsletter where I often give away free books before publication.
Join my private Facebook group where she posts exclusive excerpts and discuss all things murder and love!

Never miss a new release. Follow me on
Amazon:amazon.com/author/jentalty
And on Bookbub: bookbub.com/authors/jen-talty

ABOUT THE AUTHOR

Jen Talty is the *USA Today* Bestselling Author of Contemporary Romance, Romantic Suspense, and Paranormal Romance. In the fall of 2020, her short story was selected and featured in a 1001 Dark Nights Anthology.

Regardless of the genre, her goal is to take you on a ride that will leave you floating under the sun with warmth in your heart. She writes stories about broken heroes and heroines who aren't necessarily looking for romance, but in the end, they find the kind of love books are written about :).

She first started writing while carting her kids to one hockey rink after the other, averaging 170 games per year between 3 kids in 2 countries and 5 states. Her first book, IN TWO WEEKS was originally published in 2007. In 2010 she helped form a publishing company (Cool Gus Publishing) with *NY Times* Bestselling Author Bob Mayer where she ran the technical side of the business through 2016.

Jen is currently enjoying the next phase of her life… the empty nester! She and her husband reside in Jupiter, Florida.

Grab a glass of vino, kick back, relax, and let the romance roll in…

Sign up for my _Newsletter_ _(https://dl.bookfunnel.com/ 82gm8b9k4y)_. _where I often give away free books before publication._

Join my private _Facebook group_ _(https://www.facebook.com/ groups/191706547909047/) where I post exclusive excerpts and discuss all things murder and love!_

Never miss a new release. Follow me on Amazon:amazon.com/author/jentalty

And on Bookbub: bookbub.com/authors/jen-talty

ALSO BY JEN TALTY

Brand new series: SAFE HARBOR!

Mine To Keep

Mine To Save

Mine To Protect

Mine to Hold

Mine to Love

Check out LOVE IN THE ADIRONDACKS!

Shattered Dreams

An Inconvenient Flame

The Wedding Driver

Clear Blue Sky

Blue Moon

Before the Storm

NY STATE TROOPER SERIES (also set in the Adirondacks!)

In Two Weeks

Dark Water

Deadly Secrets

Murder in Paradise Bay

To Protect His own

Deadly Seduction

When A Stranger Calls

His Deadly Past

The Corkscrew Killer

First Responders: A spin-off from the NY State Troopers series

Playing With Fire

Private Conversation

The Right Groom

After The Fire

Caught In The Flames

Chasing The Fire

Legacy Series

Dark Legacy

Legacy of Lies

Secret Legacy

Emerald City

Investigate Away

Sail Away

Fly Away

Flirt Away

Hawaii Brotherhood Protectors

Waylen Unleashed

Bowie's Battle

Colorado Brotherhood Protectors

Fighting For Esme

Defending Raven

Fay's Six

Darius' Promise

Yellowstone Brotherhood Protectors

Guarding Payton

Wyatt's Mission

Corbin's Mission

Candlewood Falls

Rivers Edge

The Buried Secret

Its In His Kiss

Lips Of An Angel

Kisses Sweeter than Wine

A Little Bit Whiskey

It's all in the Whiskey

Johnnie Walker

Georgia Moon

Jack Daniels

Jim Beam

Whiskey Sour

Whiskey Cobbler

Whiskey Smash

Irish Whiskey

The Monroes

Color Me Yours

Color Me Smart

Color Me Free

Color Me Lucky

Color Me Ice

Color Me Home

Search and Rescue

Protecting Ainsley

Protecting Clover

Protecting Olympia

Protecting Freedom

Protecting Princess

Protecting Marlowe

Fallport Rescue Operations

Searching for Madison

Searching for Haven

Searching for Pandora

Searching for Stormi

DELTA FORCE-NEXT GENERATION

Shielding Jolene

Shielding Aalyiah

Shielding Laine

Shielding Talullah

Shielding Maribel

Shielding Daisy

The Men of Thief Lake

Rekindled

Destiny's Dream

Federal Investigators

Jane Doe's Return

The Butterfly Murders

THE AEGIS NETWORK

The Sarich Brother

The Lighthouse

Her Last Hope

The Last Flight

The Return Home

The Matriarch

Aegis Network: Jacksonville Division

A SEAL's Honor

Talon's Honor

Arthur's Honor

Rex's Honor

Kent's Honor

Buddy's Honor

Aegis Network Short Stories

Max & Milian

A Christmas Miracle

Spinning Wheels

Holiday's Vacation

The Brotherhood Protectors

Out of the Wild

Rough Justice

Rough Around The Edges

Rough Ride

Rough Edge

Rough Beauty

The Brotherhood Protectors

The Saving Series

Saving Love

Saving Magnolia

Saving Leather

Hot Hunks

Cove's Blind Date Blows Up

My Everyday Hero – Ledger

Tempting Tavor

Malachi's Mystic Assignment

Needing Neor

Holiday Romances

A Christmas Getaway

Alaskan Christmas

Whispers

Christmas In The Sand

Heroes & Heroines on the Field

Taking A Risk

Tee Time

A New Dawn

The Blind Date

Spring Fling

Summers Gone

Winter Wedding

The Awakening

Fated Moons

The Collective Order

The Lost Sister

The Lost Soldier

The Lost Soul

The Lost Connection

The New Order